crime and the economy

```
compact
criminology
```

Compact Criminology
Series editors: Nicole Rafter and Paul Rock

Compact Criminology is an exciting new series that invigorates and challenges the international field of criminology.

Books in the series are short, authoritative, innovative assessments of emerging issues in criminology and criminal justice – offering critical, accessible introductions to important topics. They take a global rather than a narrowly national approach. Eminently readable and first-rate in quality, each book is written by a leading specialist.

Compact Criminology provides a new type of tool for teaching and research, one that is flexible and light on its feet. The series is designed to address fundamental needs in the growing and increasingly differentiated field of criminology.

Other Compact Criminology titles include:

Comparing Criminal Justice by David Nelken
Crime and Risk by Pat O'Malley
Experimental Criminology by Lawrence Sherman
Crime and Terror by Michael Stohl and Peter Grabosky

Compact Criminology International Advisory Board:

Jan Van Dijk, University of Tilburg
Peter Grabosky, Australian National University
Kelly Hannah-Moffat, University of Toronto
Alison Leibling, University of Cambridge

compact
criminology

crime and the economy

Richard Rosenfeld • Steven F. Messner

SAGE

Los Angeles | London | New Delhi
Singapore | Washington DC

Los Angeles | London | New Delhi
Singapore | Washington DC

SAGE Publications Ltd
1 Oliver's Yard
55 City Road
London EC1Y 1SP

SAGE Publications Inc.
2455 Teller Road
Thousand Oaks, California 91320

SAGE Publications India Pvt Ltd
B 1/I 1 Mohan Cooperative Industrial Area
Mathura Road
New Delhi 110 044

SAGE Publications Asia-Pacific Pte Ltd
3 Church Street
#10-04 Samsung Hub
Singapore 049483

Editor: Natalie Aguilera
Editorial assistant: James Piper
Production editor: Rachel Eley
Copyeditor: Kate Harrison
Proofreader: Sharon Cawood
Indexer: Elizabeth Ball
Marketing manager: Sally Ransom
Cover design: Wendy Scott
Typeset by: C&M Digitals (P) Ltd, Chennai, India
Printed in India at Replika Press Pvt Ltd

Library of Congress Control Number: 2012941459

British Library Cataloguing in Publication data

A catalogue record for this book is available from
the British Library

ISBN 978-1-84860-716-3
ISBN 978-1-84860-717-0 (pbk)

contents

About the Authors   vi
Preface and Acknowledgements   vii

1   Through the Looking Glass: The Complex
Relationship Between Crime and the Economy   1

2   The Theoretical Toolkit of Contemporary Criminology   19

3   Bringing in Institutions: Markets, Morality, and Crime   53

4   Understanding the Economic Context of Crime
in Capitalist Societies   68

5   Implications for Policy and Social Change   98

References   120
Index   136

about the authors

Richard Rosenfeld is Curators' Professor of Criminology and Criminal Justice at the University of Missouri – St. Louis. He is co-author with Steven F. Messner of *Crime and the American Dream* (Wadsworth, 5e) and has written widely on crime trends, crime statistics, and criminological theory. He is a Fellow and past president of the American Society of Criminology.

Steven F. Messner is Distinguished Teaching Professor of Sociology at the University at Albany, SUNY. His research focuses on social institutions and crime, understanding spatial and temporal patterns of crime, and crime and social control in China. In addition to his publications in professional journals, he is co-author of *Crime and the American Dream, Perspectives on Crime and Deviance, Criminology: An Introduction Using ExplorIt*, and co-editor of *Theoretical Integration in the Study of Deviance and Crime, Crime and Social Control in a Changing China, The SAGE Handbook of Criminological Research Methods*, and *The Emergence of a New Urban China: Insiders' Perspectives*.

preface and acknowledgements

We have written this book with two interrelated objectives in mind. One, we set out to shed light on the multifaceted linkages between criminal behaviour and the structure and functioning of the economy in advanced, capitalist societies. Although the proposition that crime is influenced by economic factors might seem virtually self-evident, the nature of this influence is actually quite complex. This observation serves as the point of departure for our second overarching objective. We seek to demonstrate that the complex linkages between crime and economic factors can be best understood when viewed through the lens of an *institutional perspective*.

In Chapter 1, we present evidence to substantiate our claim that the relationship between crime and the economy is in fact quite complex. We illustrate some of the issues surrounding *causal inferences* in the study of the economy and crime, and we call attention to the critical role of theory as a guide when making inferences about causal effects. In Chapter 2, we review the dominant theoretical perspectives in contemporary criminology. These perspectives offer many valuable insights, but they are incomplete because they fail to attend sufficiently to the 'big picture', that is, to the fundamental institutional contours of societies. Recognition of these limitations paves the way for our development and application of a distinctively institutional perspective on crime and the economy in Chapter 3, where we introduce institutional-anomie theory as one attempt to link social institutions to crime. We put our theoretical perspective to work explaining the linkages between institutional dynamics and crime with concrete illustrations in Chapter 4. In the concluding chapter, we explore the implications of our institutional approach for social policy and social change.

We would like to thank Paul Rock and Nicole Rafter for their exceptionally thoughtful comments on drafts of the manuscript. All authors should have the privilege of working with such constructive consultants. We are also grateful to Natalie Aguilera at Sage for her valuable editorial guidance and assistance.

ONE

through the looking glass:
the complex relationship between
crime and the economy

Willie Sutton was a notorious bank robber. During his 40-year criminal career he allegedly stole over $2 million.[1] He spent about half of his adult life behind bars, although he managed to escape from prison twice. He is best known for his answer when asked why he robbed banks: '... because that's where the money is.' In his partly ghost-written autobiography, *Where the Money Was: The Memoirs of a Bank Robber*, Sutton denied having uttered the phrase. He credited some enterprising reporter. Nevertheless, the words attributed to him seem to contain a pearl of wisdom: when trying to understand some phenomenon, begin with the obvious. This sage advice is sometimes referred to as 'Sutton's Law'.

At first glance, the basic focus of this book – the relationship between the economy and crime – might seem particularly well suited for the application of Sutton's Law. There appears to be nothing particularly profound or surprising in the proposition that the ups and downs of the economy and criminal activity go hand in hand. It turns out, however, that Sutton's Law serves only as a useful starting point in inquiring about the economy and crime. The picture becomes murkier as we peer through the looking glass. As self-evident and straightforward as the

---

[1] http://en.wikipedia.org/wiki/Willie_Sutton. Accessed 14 February 2011.

connection between crime and the economy might seem, the relationship is actually quite complex. A half century ago, a thorough review of the academic literature concluded that 'the general relations of economic conditions and criminality are so indefinite that no clear or definite conclusions can be drawn' (Vold, 1958: 181). Our reading of the research literature is not quite as pessimistic, but we agree that the accumulated evidence defies simple conclusions.

In this book we review the research on the relationship between crime and the economy and consider the theoretical perspectives that have been advanced to explain the complexities in that relationship. We then offer our own take on the relationship, especially as it is manifested in contemporary advanced industrial societies. Our review covers all kinds of criminal acts, violent as well as property offences and so-called white-collar as well as street crimes. Our perspective on the crime–economy relationship considers the modern market economy as a *social institution* that has powerful, if not always obvious or direct, consequences for criminal activity. The key concept in our institutional analysis is the *market*: the exchange of goods and services for money.

To set the stage for the analyses to follow, it is useful to begin by considering one particularly salient outcome of the market economy, specifically, economic deprivation or poverty. Here is where Sutton's Law is most likely be invoked. To the extent that the economy has any connection with crime, it seems almost commonsensical to surmise that poor economic circumstances will promote high levels of criminal activity. Yet, as we shall see, the relationship between economic deprivation and crime proves to be more complex than it initially appears.

Socioeconomic status and street crime

The phrase 'It's the economy, stupid' was popularized during Bill Clinton's 1992 US Presidential campaign. Advisor James Carville used the phrase to focus the campaign on the recession that occurred during the Presidential term of Clinton's opponent, George H. W. Bush. 'So goes the economy, so goes the election' has become a staple of political science research on the impact of the economy on electoral politics (Dolan et al., 2008; Fair, 2009). When we look at statistics on the socio-economic status of persons caught up in the criminal justice system, economics also predict the outcome: the poor get prison.[2]

The poor are over-represented among those who are arrested for crimes, sentenced to prison, and even those who are victimized by crime. Surveys of the inmates in local jails, including persons awaiting trial and those convicted of crimes, consistently find that jail inmates have less education, higher unemployment rates, and lower incomes than the general population of adults. For example, in 2002, 44% of jail inmates did not have a high school diploma or GED, compared with 20% of the US adult population.[3] Fully 29% of the jail inmates were unemployed during the month before they were arrested, compared with an unemployment rate of 5.8% in the general population. During the month before their arrest, 59% of jail inmates had incomes less than the federal poverty threshold for a family of two; most of those did not have enough money to support themselves above the poverty line. The poverty rate for the general population was just over 12%. The socioeconomic portrait of persons convicted for serious crimes and sentenced to state and federal prisons, if anything, is even bleaker than that of inmates in local jails (Petersilia, 2003; Western, 2006).

The picture of the socioeconomic characteristics of offenders drawn from official statistics on arrest and incarceration is of course imperfect. Criminologists have long recognized that the processing of cases by criminal justice officials – from police to prosecutors to juries and judges – can introduce systematic biases, often based on socio-economic status (Cooney, 2009; Reiman and Leighton, 2009). But even 'self-report' surveys which ask persons if they have committed crimes find that those of lower socioeconomic status report greater involvement in serious violent and property crime (e.g., Loeber and Farrington, 1998).

---

[2] *The Rich Get Richer and the Poor Get Prison* is the title of Jeffrey Reiman and Paul Leighton's (2009) provocative treatment of class bias in the US criminal justice system.

[3] The figures for jail inmates are from James (2004). The general population figures are from the 2000 Census (http://factfinder.census.gov/home/saff/main.html?_lang=en). Accessed 21 February 2011.

Another vantage point from which to observe the relationship between socioeconomic status and crime is through an examination of criminal victimization. Residential patterns in the US tend to be segregated by class (and race). In addition, criminological researchers have documented that offenders tend not to travel far from home when selecting their targets for victimization (Brantingham and Brantingham, 1993; Chainey and Ratcliffe, 2005). It is therefore not surprising that persons who live in close proximity to criminal offenders tend to have higher rates of victimization, regardless of their lifestyle and other characteristics (Sampson and Lauritsen, 1990). If socioeconomic status is in fact associated with criminal offending, we would expect that low-income residents will be at comparatively high risk of victimization.

Some evidence supports this hypothesis. Each year, the US Bureau of Justice Statistics, in conjunction with the Census Bureau, conducts an ambitious data collection effort, the National Crime Victimization Survey (NCVS). The NCVS asks representative samples of the population, age 12 and older, whether they have been the victim of a crime during the past six months and, if so, what type of crime. The NCVS also collects information on the characteristics of the households in the sample, including household income. Table 1.1 reports the burglary victimization rates per 1,000 households in 2009 according to household income. The data reveal a clear negative relationship between household income and burglary. The lowest two income categories exhibit the highest burglary rates, and the rates decline steadily as incomes rise.

Whether we look at official statistics on arrest and incarceration, self-report studies of criminal offending, or surveys of crime victims, the same pattern emerges: lower socioeconomic status is associated with greater involvement with the criminal justice system, higher rates of criminal offending, and higher rates of various forms of victimization. The relationship between socioeconomic deprivation and involvement in crime and the justice system holds not only for individuals, as we have seen, but also for neighbourhoods. Extensive research confirms the perception of nearly all urban residents: there are readily identifiable 'bad' neighbourhoods where the risk of becoming a victim of crime is high. These neighbourhoods are typically characterized by a host of disadvantages, including pervasive poverty.

Table 1.1 NCVS Burglary Rates per 1,000 Households, 2009

Under $7,500	44.4
$7,500 to $14,999	46.3
$15,000 to $24,999	35.3
$25,000 to $34,999	32.3
$35,000 to $49,999	26.7
$50,000 to $74,999	19.3
$75,000 and over	15.1

Source: Truman and Rand, 2010

An example comes from research on the city of St. Louis (Rosenfeld et al., 1999). The map displayed in Figure 1.1 divides the city into 588 census 'block groups', small geographic areas with an average population of 675 residents per block group. The block groups are shaded according to their score on an index of disadvantage, consisting of the rate of poverty, public assistance income, and female-headed households in each block group in 1990. The dark-shaded areas have very high levels of disadvantage, the lighter-shaded areas exhibit moderate levels of disadvantage, and the areas with no shading are the least disadvantaged. Superimposed on the block groups are crosses and circles representing homicides committed between 1985 and 1995, coded as 'gang-motivated' and 'gang-affiliated', respectively. The researchers defined a homicide as gang-motivated if it resulted from gang behaviour or relationships, such as an initiation ritual, the 'throwing' of gang signs, or a gang fight. A homicide was defined as gang-affiliated if it involved a suspect or victim who was a gang member but did not arise from gang activity.

Regardless of the type of homicide, the map reveals a striking association between an area's level of disadvantage and the frequency of killings. Homicides are heavily concentrated in the northern section of the city, where socioeconomic disadvantage is most pronounced, and are virtually absent in the least disadvantaged southwestern neighbourhoods.

Gang-Affiliated and Gang-Motivated Homicides
o Gang Affiliated
+ Gang Motivated
St. Louis Block Groups
▢ Not Disadvantaged
▰ Disadvantaged
▨ Very Disadvantaged

2   0   2   4 Miles   N

Figure 1.1   The Relationship Between Gang Homicides and Neighbourhood Socioeconomic Disadvantage in St. Louis, 1985–95.

Source: Rosenfeld et al., 1999

St. Louis is not alone in exhibiting this strong spatial association
between gang homicides and socioeconomic disadvantage. Nor is the
relationship between disadvantage and crime confined to homicides or
gang crimes. A century of research on neighbourhoods and crime

consistently reveals the same pattern: crime tends to be concentrated in disadvantaged places (Bursik and Grasmick, 1993; Pratt and Cullen, 2005; Sampson et al., 2002).

The evidence presented thus far would seem to confirm the obvious: there is a straightforward relationship between crime and economic outcomes. Low socioeconomic status is associated with increased risk of criminal offending and victimization, and thus by extension, the level of criminal activity should reflect the extent to which the economy effectively 'delivers the goods' in society. It turns out, however, that the relationship between economic conditions and crime – even crimes committed for economic gain – is more complex than it appears at first glance. To understand these complexities, it is necessary to introduce some important conceptual and analytic distinctions.

Complicating the picture

Up to this point, we have framed the basic topic of inquiry for this book in rather loose language, by referring to the 'relationship' between the economy and crime. Our illustrations of a definite connection between socioeconomic deprivation and crime have in fact been based on empirical relationships and the statistical associations that represent them. However, such associations are typically of interest insofar as they allow us to make inferences about the presence and nature of *causal* processes. Do features of the economy actually produce or inhibit criminal activity in meaningful ways, and if so, how? It turns out that drawing causal inferences on the basis of empirical associations is a highly challenging task that ultimately requires theoretical guidance.

A full exposition of the intricacies of causal inference goes well beyond the scope of our discussion, but we can indicate here some of the complexities of interpreting statistical associations with illustrations from criminological research. This will serve as a useful starting point for our investigation into the complex relationship between crime and the economy. Figure 1.2 displays different processes that might conceivably link outcomes of the economy with some indicator of criminal activity. Panel A depicts a direct effect of an economic outcome on crime. In the language of causal modelling, such an effect is referred to as 'unmediated'. It does not operate in conjunction with any other identified variable. If the economic factor were the only one to influence crime (which is implausible), and if we were to measure the variables well, the simple statistical association between these variables would serve as an impeccable guide to any underlying causal effect.

Panel B elaborates the causal model by introducing an additional factor, indicated by variable 'Z'. This model depicts a causal process wherein the effect of an economic outcome comes about by virtue of its effect on Z, which in turn affects crime. Panel C is also a model that entails mediating causal processes, but with two mediating factors at work. Both of these models depict scenarios in which underlying causal processes might not be readily apparent in the simple, overall statistical association between an economic outcome and an indicator of criminal activity.

Panel D illustrates a fourth scenario: a conditional relationship between an outcome of the economy and crime. The arrow to the arrow in the diagram implies that the effect of the economic factor differs depending on the third variable. This third variable is usually referred to as a 'moderating' variable. It moderates the relationship between the other two variables.

Finally, Panel E introduces another complicating factor: the level of aggregation of the units of analysis ('level of analysis', for short). In much research, individuals serve as the units of interest, but as we have seen in the example of homicide and neighbourhood disadvantage, it is also possible to theorize about individuals aggregated into meaningful social groupings. This aggregation can range from small groups (e.g., families) to larger communities (e.g., neighbourhoods) to whole societies. As such, an important issue to consider is the extent to which any statistical relationship found at a given level of analysis, such as that of individuals, can be directly translated to another level.

Even as we begin to complicate the relationship between crime and the economy, the scenarios presented in Figure 1.2 represent only a few of the possible complexities. We have depicted the relationship between crime and the economy with single-headed arrows, as if the economy influences crime, but not the reverse. But research has shown that the criminal propensities of individuals and the crime rates of communities can affect their economic status – usually for the worse. The causal relationship between crime and the economy, in other words, is likely to be a two-way street. In addition, Figure 1.2 does not indicate whether the variables are observed at a single point in time or over multiple time points. The former type of analysis is referred to as *cross-sectional* and the latter type as *longitudinal* analysis. We shall see that the results of cross-sectional and longitudinal research often differ; sometimes they produce contradictory conclusions regarding the strength or direction of the crime–economy relationship.

The scenarios shown in Figure 1.2, however, offer a useful starting point for our investigation into the complex relationship between crime and the economy. We take up the additional complexities in the following chapters. Here we illustrate scenarios of mediating and moderating effects, and the issue of levels of analysis, with data and research that describe the association between crime and economic conditions across nations and over time within the United States. We begin by presenting data and research relevant to mediating processes.

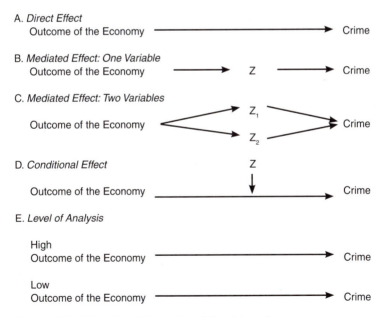

Figure 1.2   Five Causal Scenarios of the Crime–Economy Relationship.

Is the relationship between the economy and violent crime mediated by property crime?

If economic conditions influence crime rates, it is reasonable to expect that they should have stronger or more immediate effects on property crimes, which are committed for economic gain, than on violent crimes, which often seem to have little to do with economic considerations. Throughout history, people have been assaulted and killed for all kinds of reasons and not simply for their money or property. When violence is used for economic gain, the crime is termed a 'robbery' – theft accompanied by force or the threat of force. In essence, robbers apply the means of violent crime (force) to the ends of property crime (material acquisition). Recent research supports the expectation that economic conditions have a robust statistical association with temporal change in property crimes and little or no association with trends in violent crimes, other than robbery (e.g., Arvanites and Defina, 2006).

Should we then conclude that violent crime has no meaningful causal connection with changing economic conditions? Prior research would support that conclusion, but only if the impact of the economy on violent crime is assumed to be unmediated, that is, takes the form of the simple relationship depicted by the diagram in Panel A of Figure 1.2. Yet there are good reasons to suppose that the economy influences violent crimes indirectly, that is, through its effect on other conditions that, in turn, affect the rate of violent crime, as depicted in Panel B of Figure 1.2. A recent study proposed that an important mediator of the relationship between violent crime and the economy is property crime (Rosenfeld, 2009).

If this hypothesis is correct, we should observe a positive relationship between rates of violent crime and crimes committed for economic gain. Figure 1.3 displays the trends between 1970 and 2006 in homicide, the most serious violent crime, and an index of 'acquisitive crime' in the United States. Acquisitive crime is defined as criminal offences intended to acquire money or valuables from the victim and in this example consists of the combined rates of robbery, burglary, and motor vehicle theft (Rosenfeld, 2009). The annual rates of homicide and acquisitive crime are shown in Panel A of the figure. Panel B displays the year-over-year changes in the rates (i.e., each year's rate minus the previous year's rate). In both cases, we see a strong correspondence between the two series, as

A. Homicide and Acquisitive Crime Rates

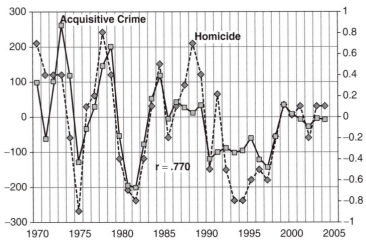

B. Year-over-Year Change in Homicide and Acquisitive Crime Rates

Figure 1.3 Rates of Homicide and Acquisitive Crime per 100,000 Population, 1970–2006.

Source: Rosenfeld, 2009

revealed by the sizable correlations (r) shown in the figure. [4] Whether expressed as annual rates or changes, when acquisitive crime rises, homicide tends to increase as well. When acquisitive crime declines, so does homicide. There are exceptions, especially in the late 1980s and early 1990s, when homicide increases outpaced those in acquisitive crime but, in general, the 27-year trends in homicide and acquisitive crime shown in Figure 1.3 track one another rather closely.

Correlation, of course, does not necessarily mean causation. In Chapter 4, we present arguments and evidence to support the hypothesis that violent and property crimes are in fact causally related to one another. For now, we suggest only that the case for assuming that economic conditions are unrelated to violent crime may have been closed prematurely if the relationship between the economy and violent crime is mediated by property crime or some other condition.

Might causal processes linking the economy and crime work in opposing directions?

When making our initial case for a relationship between socioeconomic status and crime, we cited evidence of a distinct inverse relationship between household income and the risk of victimization for burglary. We were actually being selective in our use of the evidence for didactic purposes. It turns out that we could have drawn a different portrait if we had chosen to consider a different form of property crime, referred to as 'theft' – the illegal taking of property from the custody or care of another person without force or breaking and entering. Table 1.2 presents victimization rates for theft by household income based on the data from the NCVS. Similar to the case for burglary, the lowest income category exhibits a relatively high victimization rate (150.7), which decreases along with increasing income up to a point. But then victimization rates increase with higher incomes, and the highest income category ($75,000 and over) has a victimization rate greater

---

[4] The correlation coefficient (r) measures the strength of the linear statistical association between two variables and takes on values between minus one and one. A value of zero indicates no relationship between the variables. Values close to one indicate a strong positive relationship; those close to minus one indicate a strong negative relationship.

Table 1.2 NCVS Theft Rates per 1,000 Households, 2009

Under $7,500	150.7
$7,500 to $14,999	102.4
$15,000 to $24,999	99.8
$25,000 to $34,999	95.3
$35,000 to $49,999	102.8
$50,000 to $74,999	96.2
$75,000 and over	105.6

Source: Truman and Rand, 2010

than those for the other categories, except for the very lowest. Overall, there is no simple linear relationship between the two variables.

Why might those in the highest income group have a risk of being victimized by theft? Applying Sutton's Law, the answer might seem obvious: they have the money. Yet this does not explain why the relationship between household income and the victimization risk for theft is not consistently positive: the higher the income, the higher the risk. As an initial step in interpreting the lack of any distinct relationship between household income and theft, it is useful to consider Panel C in Figure 1.2. Perhaps household income, as an outcome of the economy, is causally related to this form of property crime through two different processes, which operate in opposing directions. Members of low-income households are likely to have greater exposure to potential criminals, but they also tend to have less valuable property to steal. The reverse is true for members of high-income households. Such countervailing mediating effects might explain why neither a positive nor negative statistical association emerges for measures of economic outcomes and theft, even though there are important causal processes at work.[5]

---

[5] In Chapter 2, we review 'routine activities' theory, which introduces another factor that is related to both household income and victimization risk for property crimes: 'guardianship'. Routine activities theory offers an account for why economic factors such as household income might be related to different types of property crime in different ways.

Is the relationship between unemployment and homicide moderated by the welfare state?

As we have seen, prior research reveals a weak or null relationship between economic conditions and violent crimes, with the exception of robbery. We have proposed that the relationship may be mediated by crimes committed for economic gain, which are influenced by the economy and, in turn, have an effect on violent crime. We now propose an additional scenario for understanding the link between economic conditions and violent crime: the relationship is moderated by the size and scope of social welfare provisions which nations provide for their citizens. This is the scenario depicted in Panel D of Figure 1.2. We investigate this hypothesis in some detail in Chapter 4. Here, we illustrate the moderating hypothesis with the results of a study we conducted that show how unemployment can have differing effects on the homicide rates of nations depending on the generosity of their welfare states (Rosenfeld and Messner, 2007).

We surmised that the strength of the relationship between national economic conditions and violent crime depends on the degree to which nations protect their citizens from the full brunt of market forces. In countries that provide their citizens with extensive unemployment insurance, health insurance and pensions, the impact of market forces on crime should be weaker than in those with less generous social welfare provisions. We evaluated this hypothesis with data on the unemployment rates, homicide rates, social welfare benefits, and other conditions for 13 advanced industrial nations over the period 1971 to 2001. An initial task was to document that these nations did in fact differ in the size and scope of their social welfare provisions. We took our measure of welfare generosity from the Comparative Welfare Entitlements Dataset, which scores nations according to the universality and extensiveness of their unemployment, sickness, and pension benefits (Scruggs, 2004). Figure 1.4 rank orders the 13 nations in our study by this measure.

Figure 1.4 reveals substantial variation across the 13 nations in the generosity of their social welfare provisions. The welfare systems in Sweden and Norway, for example, are more than twice as generous as those in the United Kingdom, the United States and Japan. The next

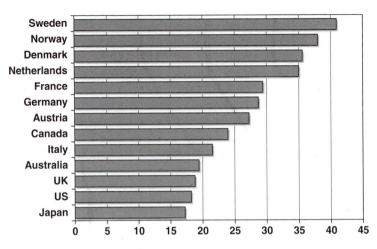

Figure 1.4 Average Welfare Generosity in 13 Nations, 1971–2001.

Source: Rosenfeld and Messner, 2007; Scruggs, 2004

question is whether these differences moderate the effect of unemployment on the homicide rates of the 13 nations between 1971 and 2001.

One simple test of the moderating hypothesis is to divide the nations into two groups according to whether they score above or below the average value on the welfare generosity index and conduct a separate analysis of the relationship between unemployment and homicide rates over the 32-year period within each group. When we did this, we found no statistically significant effect of unemployment on homicide for the nations scoring above average on the welfare generosity index. By contrast, we found a statistically significant and positive effect of unemployment on homicide for the lower scoring nations. In these nations, higher rates of unemployment were associated with higher homicide rates. These results were confirmed when we applied a more sophisticated statistical model to the data. In short, consistent with the type of causal process depicted in Panel D of Figure 1.2, the relationship between unemployment and homicide evidently depends, at least in part, on the size and scope of a nation's social welfare system.

Are relationships between economic outcomes and crime always translatable across different levels of analysis?

We saw earlier that the risk of burglary (but not theft) varies inversely with household income. As household income rises, burglary victimization rates decline steadily. When extrapolated to the national level, we might expect that burglary rates would be lowest in those nations that have achieved the highest level of affluence. Figure 1.5 plots the residential burglary rate against the per capita gross domestic product for nine European nations and the United States in the year 2000. The gross domestic product (GDP) measures the total value of goods and

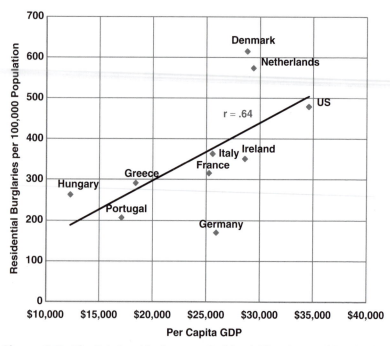

Figure 1.5   The Relationship Between Residential Burglary and Per Capita GDP in 10 Nations, 2000.

Source: Eurostat, Uniform Crime Reports[1]

[1] Eurostat: http://epp.eurostat.ec.europa.eu/portal/page/portal/eurostat/home. Uniform Crime Reports: http://www.fbi.gov/about-us/cjis/ucr/ucr. Accessed 3 February 2011.

services produced by a nation and is a good indicator of general afflu-ence. The figure reveals a definite statistical association, but the sign of the relationship is positive rather than negative. Although the relation-ship is far from perfect ($r = .64$), nations with higher per capita GDP generally tend to have *higher* residential burglary rates.

How can we reconcile these seemingly contradictory findings regard-ing the relationship between burglary and income among households and burglary and affluence across nations? Why should high burglary rates coincide with low household income but also with high national affluence? There are many possible reasons for this apparent discrep-ancy, in part because many possible *mechanisms* may account for the effect of economic conditions on burglary rates. As alluded to above and developed more fully in the next chapter, criminological theory suggests that some of these mechanisms will produce a negative rela-tionship and some will produce a positive relationship between eco-nomic outcomes and crime. The direction of the relationship, then, may depend on which of the hypothesized mechanisms is most impor-tant. It follows that the mechanisms producing the negative relation-ship between burglary and household income are likely to differ from those producing the positive relationship between burglary and national affluence.

Summary and the chapters ahead

Despite ample indications that economic considerations may be a source of personal distress and criminal behaviour, research on the relationship between crime and the economy tells a more complex story. We saw that socioeconomic status tends to be negatively associ-ated with criminal behaviour, victimization, and involvement with the criminal justice system – at least for serious street crimes such as bur-glary and homicide. Later, when we consider the so-called white-collar crimes committed by persons who occupy corporate suites or govern-ment bureaus, the relationship between socioeconomic position and criminal behaviour looks very different.

But even the association between economic conditions and street crime turns out to be more complex than it first appears. To unravel these complexities, we called attention to the important conceptual distinction between statistical associations and causal relationships, and we illustrated some of the difficulties associated with drawing causal inferences with reference to five causal scenarios. The common feature of all but the first of these scenarios is that they depict mechanisms that describe *how* crime and economic conditions might be related to one another. We have invoked two scenarios that depict mediating mechanisms. We illustrated one mediating scenario with evidence showing the close association between homicide and 'acquisitive' crimes and suggested that such crimes committed for economic gain may mediate the association between violent crime and the economy. The second mediating scenario entails mediating causal processes that work in opposite directions. Such opposing or countervailing processes provide a plausible account for the lack of any clear statistical relationship between socioeconomic status and the risk of personal theft, even though meaningful causal processes are at work.

A close cousin to the mediating scenarios is the moderating scenario. This scenario depicts the relationship between crime and economic conditions as dependent on the presence or strength of some third condition. In an example from our own research, we presented evidence that the relationship between unemployment and burglary is moderated by the strength of the welfare state. Finally, we introduced the issue of extrapolating observed relationships from one level of analysis, such as individual persons or households, to relationships that might pertain to social aggregates. We reported evidence revealing a positive association between a measure of affluence and levels of burglary based on data for a sample of nation states that is the opposite of the negative relationship typically observed in research on individual economic status and burglary victimization.

These are just a few of the complexities uncovered by research on crime and the economy.[6] Making sense of the complex association between individual economic status and criminal behaviour, and aggregate economic conditions and the crime rates of communities or whole societies, is the job of criminological theory. In the following chapter, we discuss the major criminological perspectives that have been used to explain the manifold connections between crime and the economy.

---

[6] See Crutchfield (forthcoming) for an extensive discussion of the link between the nature and quality of employment and crime.

TWO

the theoretical toolkit of contemporary criminology

A common refrain in everyday arguments goes something like this: 'I hear what you say, but that's only a theory'. Such a statement reflects a fundamental misunderstanding of the role of theory. It relegates theory to second-class status by implying that theoretical knowledge is inferior to some other type of knowledge, perhaps knowledge of the 'facts'. Yet philosophers of science have extolled the virtues of theory, explaining that good theories not only account for widely observed regularities in the world around us – the 'facts' – they also 'afford a deeper and more accurate understanding of the phenomena in question' (Hempel, 1966: 70). Indeed, the distinguishing feature of a mature scientific discipline is precisely its theoretical sophistication.

Criminology is a relatively young field of inquiry, and thus its theoretical accomplishments have been modest to date, certainly in comparison with those in the natural sciences. Nevertheless, various criminological theories have been developed to provide a deeper and more accurate understanding of the causes of crime. In any serious effort to explain the complex role of the economy in the production of crime, it is thus essential to traverse the theoretical terrain of criminology.

In this chapter, we describe the commonly used criminological perspectives that help to understand the relationship between crime and the economy. We begin by introducing an overarching analytic framework that is general enough to encompass the range of processes that have been cited in the different theoretical perspectives. We then summarize the core arguments of the major theories and illustrate how each can be invoked to establish causal linkages between various aspects of the functioning of the economy and levels and patterns of crime. These theoretical perspectives offer many valuable insights, but they are incomplete in a fundamental respect. They fail to attend sufficiently to the 'big picture', that is, to the fundamental institutional contours of large-scale social systems.[1] Recognition of these limitations paves the way for our development and application of a distinctively institutional perspective on crime and the economy in later chapters.

Unpacking mechanisms: theoretical linkages between the economy and crime

In Chapter 1, we introduced several causal models to help guide inter-pretations of the linkages between the economy and crime. These models were cast in highly abstract terms. They indicated the general types of causal processes that could conceivably be operating. The primary contribution of criminological theories is to provide the substantive content for such abstract models. These theories attempt to explain why crimes are committed, who commits them, how prevalent criminal events are likely to be, and where they are likely to occur. As even a casual perusal of any textbook will reveal, there is no shortage of theorizing about the causes of crime in criminology. Indeed, at times the field might seem to be plagued by an embarrassment of riches, populated with a baffling array of theoretical arguments.

Despite the voluminous literature on the causes of crime, the core insights of criminological theories can be captured reasonably well by a straightforward and parsimonious analytic framework. Criminological theories can be subdivided, roughly, into perspectives that seek to explain the *motivations* to engage in crime, the *controls* (or constraints) that impede or reduce criminal behaviour, and/or the *opportunities* to commit crime. It is useful to conceive of motivations, controls, and

[1] Some phenomenological sociologists believe that 'social systems' and 'institutions' do not exist or, if they do exist, cannot be apprehended with standard research methods. We disagree and are convinced that the concepts of institutions and social systems are indispensable for any satisfactory explanation of social phenomena. For an extended discussion of the historical development of social institutions, see Turner (2003).

opportunities as necessary conditions or requisites for criminal behaviour. The functioning of the economy ultimately becomes relevant to understanding crime because of its interconnections with the requisites of crime: motivations, controls, and opportunities. Our integrated analytic framework is presented schematically in Figure 2.1.

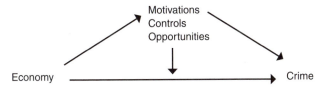

Motivations
Controls
Opportunities

Economy ——————————————————→ Crime

Figure 2.1 An Integrated Analytic Framework of the Linkages Between the Economy and Crime.

Using the language of Chapter 1, motivations, controls, and opportunities serve as potential mediators between any personal or social conditions and crime. The functioning of the economy can thus affect crime in part because it stimulates or suppresses criminal motivations, weakens or bolsters controls, or amplifies or reduces criminal opportunities. Our diagram also depicts an 'arrow to an arrow' which, as explained in the previous chapter, signifies moderating effects. The strength or direction of the effect of the economy on crime may depend on the presence of criminal opportunities and the potency of criminal motivations and controls. In the sections that follow, we describe how the major criminological theories have established linkages among the economy, the requisites of crime, and criminal behaviour. Our discussion is organized around the two principal levels of analysis that have guided the bulk of criminological theorizing and research: the individual level and the level of the local neighbourhood or community.

The individual level of analysis: rational choice and criminal decision-making

No matter how 'macro' their orientation, all criminological perspectives contain assumptions about the nature of criminal decision-making.

Some perspectives treat the problem of criminal decision-making only implicitly, while in others decision-making is the explicit theoretical focus. The dominant orientation to decision-making in the study of the economy and crime focuses on *rational choice*: actors appraise behavioural alternatives for pursuing self-interest in terms of their respective costs and benefits. This perspective was brought into the study of the economy and crime in the modern era by the economist Gary Becker (1968). Other economists, notably Isaac Ehrlich (1973), developed important elaborations and applications of the perspective.

The conception of human nature underlying the rational-choice perspective seems simple enough and should be familiar: human beings tend to act in what they perceive to be their own best interests. In the economists' terms, human beings seek to maximize their utility, which is another way of saying that, on average, we make choices that we believe will best serve our interests, preferences, or desires. As straightforward and self-evident as this proposition seems, it has profound implications for the study of human behaviour. The entire edifice of modern economics is built on it and would be utterly unrecognizable without it.

The rational-choice perspective also contributed to the development of criminology as a field of systematic scholarly inquiry. Two of the founding fathers of criminology, Jeremy Bentham (1996 [1789]) and Cesare Beccaria (1995 [1766]), applied utilitarian philosophical principles to the study of crime and punishment. Utilitarian thought holds that human beings seek pleasure and try to avoid pain. Furthermore, the ideal society is one that produces the greatest good for the greatest number. Just and efficient punishment, from this perspective, has the following characteristics: it involves only enough pain to deter criminal behaviour; it should be proportionate to the seriousness of the offence; and it should be applied swiftly, publicly, and with certainty (Beccaria 1995 [1766]).

The economist Isaac Ehrlich (1973) developed a formal model that relates crime rates to economic conditions by way of the utilitarian calculus. It is worth quoting Ehrlich at some length regarding the decision to commit crime because he explicitly contrasts the rational-choice perspective with criminological theories that posit a 'unique' criminal motivation.

Much of the search in the criminological literature for a theory explaining participation in illegitimate activities seems to have been guided by the predisposition that since crime is a deviant behavior, its causes must be sought in deviant factors and circumstances determining behavior. Criminal behavior has traditionally been linked to the offender's presumed unique motivation which, in turn, has been traced to his presumed unique inner structure, to the impact of exceptional social or family circumstances, or to both. ... Our alternative point of reference, although not necessarily incompatible, is that even if those who violate certain laws differ systematically in various respects from those who abide by the same laws, the former, like the latter, do respond to incentives. (1973: 522)

Ehrlich (1973) is asserting that the common thread uniting criminals and law-abiding persons is that both 'respond to incentives', that is, they take advantage of opportunities to serve or advance their interests. For the rational-choice theorist, and for the purposes of argument, criminals and non-criminals are not qualitatively different types of people. The choice to commit or refrain from crime is available to everyone, and everyone makes the choice based on a calculation, however imperfect, of costs and benefits. Persons decide to commit crime, says Ehrlich, in the same way they choose an occupation, on the basis of the benefits or rewards it offers in comparison with alternatives (1973: 522).

The economists' version of the rational-choice perspective provides a simple but powerful explanation of the choice to commit crime: crime pays. If it did not – if its costs relative to alternatives outweighed its benefits – it would seem to be irrational to choose crime over other ways of satisfying one's interests, preferences, and desires. And for the economist, most people, most of the time, behave rationally in light of the information available to them and the uncertainties and risks inherent in most choices. But the very emphasis on rational choice has opened the perspective to multiple criticisms and led to extensions and reformulations. Perhaps the most basic criticism concerns the absence of *moral* considerations in the choice to commit or refrain from crime. It takes only a moment's reflection to conclude that we often act on the basis of considerations of right and wrong and not simply in terms of self-interest. And what of habitual behaviour, which by definition involves no conscious choice-making at all? Or behaviour that responds to the expectations of others whose opinions we value, such as parents, spouses, and peers? Finally, what are the criteria for determining whether a given behaviour is 'rational'? Where do these standards come from? How are they acquired?

A common response to such criticisms invokes the concept of 'psychic rewards'. Because psychic rewards include any and all non-pecuniary behavioural benefits, even behaviours that result in economic loss, such as charitable giving or acts of heroism, may be viewed as rewarding and therefore consistent with the rational-choice perspective. Unless one is careful, however, this kind of reasoning can become circular. *Any* choice can be viewed as rational because it is assumed to satisfy a psychic need or preference. Indeed, the very making of the choice itself might be taken as evidence of an expected psychic reward.

Philosophers and social scientists have worried over this logical conundrum in rational-choice theory for more than a century. Few social scientists reject the idea that people tend to behave in accordance with their interests. But they have sought to specify in some detail the historical conditions that establish the standards for rational conduct and the social contexts in which rational choices are made. The essence of this approach to rational choice is captured in Marx's comment on history-making in the *Eighteenth Brumaire of Louis Bonaparte* (Marx and Engels, 1969 [1852]): 'Men [and women] make their own history, but they do not make it just as they please; they do not make it under circumstances chosen by themselves, but under circumstances directly encountered, given and transmitted from the past' (p. 398).

Extensions and reformulations of the rational-choice perspective

Over a half century ago, the sociologist Dennis Wrong (1961) wrote an important paper criticizing what he called the 'oversocialized' conception of human behaviour in modern sociology. Wrong argued that sociological theory had created a caricature of human behaviour as fully determined by social forces beyond the control of individuals. The rational-choice perspective may be seen as an antidote to such an over-socialized conception of behaviour. But rational choice, if taken to extremes, errs in the opposite direction, toward an under-socialized view of human action that is insufficiently informed by core insights from social anthropology, sociology, and social psychology. Recent criminological extensions of the rational-choice perspective have sought to correct this tendency by specifying the non-rational bases of human decision-making. Some of the recent theorizing remains squarely within the rational-choice tradition and simply extends the perspective to encompass the social sources of individual decision-making or the contexts to which the perspective can be fruitfully applied. Other work, however, reformulates the rational-choice perspective by empha-sizing the non-rational constraints on the decision to commit or refrain from crime.

Derek Cornish and Ronald Clarke (1986) deserve much credit for bringing the rational-choice perspective into contemporary criminol-ogy. As Ehrlich (1973) had before them, Cornish and Clarke contend that criminologists have devoted far too much attention to the psycho-logical and social factors that presumably distinguish criminals from non-criminals, and too little attention to the rational basis for criminal behaviour and the situational contingencies that make crime a more or less attractive behavioural choice. Not surprisingly, the rational-choice perspective is the theoretical inspiration for crime-control strategies, such as situational crime prevention, that seek to reduce crime by alter-ing *crime settings* to make the commission of crime more difficult and potentially more costly. Each time you lock the door after leaving your apartment or car, or leave the lights on at home when you are away, you are engaging in situational crime prevention. The point is to reduce the opportunities and raise the costs of crime commission to such an extent that the rational individual will choose to avoid crime (see Clarke, 1997).

A somewhat different perspective that nonetheless retains the basic assumption of rational choice is Michael Gottfredson's and Travis Hirschi's general theory of crime. Gottfredson and Hirschi (1990) focus on the offender as well as the offence. The primary individual trait that leads to criminal behaviour, they say, is *low self-control*. Low self-control is manifested in impulsivity, an orientation to the here and now, and insensitivity to the needs of others. Persons who lack adequate self-control seek out immediate pleasures and will engage in force or fraud, if necessary, to satisfy their desires. Only the absence of opportunity will deter them from crime, if they believe crime will advance their interests.

Persons who lack self-control are rational actors, although their impulsivity may result in hasty and ill-informed decisions. Individuals who are capable of exercising self-control, on the other hand, rarely engage in criminal behaviour, even, presumably, when it would serve their interests to do so. Although this does not mean that high self-control necessarily leads to irrational behaviour, it does distinguish Gottfredson and Hirschi's general theory from other rational-choice perspectives. For Gottfredson and Hirschi, self-control conditions the effect of the rational calculation of costs and rewards on the decision to engage in crime. Persons with high self-control will refrain from crime regardless of how favourable the cost–benefit ratio may be. Those with low self-control will exploit any and all opportunities, criminal or otherwise, to advance their interests. We might think of Gottfredson and Hirschi's theory as a conditional or 'bounded' theory of rational choice, with self-control limiting the full and free exercise of rational calculation in the decision to commit crime.[2]

A different approach to decision-making from social psychology incorporates non-rational factors into the framework. These perspectives propose that rational action is strongly conditioned by biosocial impediments or constraints (e.g., Beaver, 2009; Beaver and Connolly, 2011), social learning (Akers, 1998), strain (Agnew, 2006), social control (Hirschi, 1969), or some combination of these factors. A final perspective, Wikström's (2006, 2010) situational-action theory, considers the decision to commit crime as a fundamentally moral choice made in the context of situational contingencies.

Biological perspectives on crime have a long and controversial history (see Rafter, 1997, 2008). The early eighteenth century 'phrenologists' believed they could discover criminal traits and tendencies by examining the shape of an individual's skull. Biological theories of criminal behaviour entered the scientific era in the late nineteenth century in the work of Italian criminologist, Cesare Lombroso.

---

[2] See Goode (2008) and Pratt and Cullen (2000) for theoretical and empirical assessments of Gottfredson and Hirschi's (1990) general theory of crime.

Lombroso held that 'born criminals' were atavistic throwbacks to more primitive forms of humanity and could be detected by their sloped foreheads, protruding jaws, and other anatomical abnormalities. Later theories attributed criminality to inherited imbecility or to particular body types. None of these theories has survived modern scientific scrutiny, but biological perspectives on criminal behaviour have not gone away. Indeed, in recent years they have experienced something of a comeback, albeit in much more sophisticated form than their nineteenth and early twentieth century predecessors.

The current theories propose that much criminal or antisocial behaviour is a product of the interaction of biological traits and environmental adversity (Beaver and Connolly, 2011; Moffitt, 2005b). Many biological traits have been implicated, not all of which are genetic in origin (i.e., heritable). These theories do not imply that criminal behaviour is intrinsically non-rational. Rather, they suggest that the choice to engage in or refrain from criminal behaviour is conditioned by both biological and social-environmental influences, and their interaction.

Like the contemporary biosocial perspectives, *social learning, strain,* and *social control* theories seek to explain individual differences in criminal behaviour. According to current social learning theories, individuals will engage in criminal behaviour depending on the amount, frequency, and probability of its reinforcement (Burgess and Akers, 1966). Derived from behavioural psychology, the concept of reinforcement explains behaviour in terms of its consequences. Behaviour that results in positive consequences for the individual is said to be positively reinforced and is likely to be repeated. Similarly, behaviour that enables the individual to avoid an unpleasant consequence is said to be negatively reinforced and is also likely to be repeated. Behaviour that results in undesirable consequences, such as punishment, is less likely to be repeated. Much criminal behaviour, according to social learning theory, is positively reinforced by groups of like-minded others, although it may also be reinforced by exposure to reference groups in which the individual does not participate or by exposure to media presentations.

In one important respect, Aker's social learning theory bears a close resemblance to the rational-choice perspective. Social learning theory holds that individuals will repeat behaviours with positive consequences ('rewards') and avoid those with negative consequences ('costs'). But the picture of the individual that emerges from social learning theory is not that of an active and conscious calculator of the costs and benefits of alternative behavioural choices. The precursors of crime may have occurred long before a given criminal act and have been so continuously or thoroughly reinforced that the criminal act does not appear to be a 'choice' at all. From the social learning perspective, the so-called choice to engage in or refrain from crime is heavily conditioned by the individual's past and present social environment, and in particular by reference groups and their associated behavioural standards.

Another theoretical perspective that highlights the role of the social environment in conditioning the exercise of rational decision-making is Robert Agnew's (2006) *general strain theory*. General strain theory explains criminal behaviour as a coping mechanism when individuals fail to achieve positively valued goals (e.g., expected social or economic rewards); are presented with negative stimuli (e.g., child abuse or criminal victimization); or have positively valued stimuli removed (e.g., in the loss of a friend or family member). By engaging in criminal or other deviant behaviour, persons attempt to achieve goals through illegitimate means, reduce the source or consequences of negative stimuli, or replace the loss of positive stimuli.[3] Of the social psychological theories of criminal behaviour considered in this chapter, Agnew's general strain theory has the least in common with rational-choice perspectives. The criminal or deviant in Agnew's theory is someone beset by frustration, anger, depression, or despair – 'stressed out' in contemporary parlance – and trying whatever he or she can to cope. This is certainly not the image of the calculating, optimizing, reasoning criminal found in economic and rational-choice theories.

Yet, Agnew adds an essential element to such conceptions of the rational actor and to the other social-psychological theories under consideration: the role of emotions. Strong emotional states, perhaps especially anger, may cloud thinking and lead to behaviours that the individual, in a different frame of mind, would avoid. The same is true

---

[3] General strain theory was developed as a social psychological counterpart to, and elaboration of, the anomie perspective on crime associated with Robert Merton (1968). We discuss the relationship between economic conditions and anomie in Chapter 4.

of alcohol and drug abuse as coping mechanisms for strain. Agnew's general strain theory serves as an important reminder that emotions may condition the effect of the rational calculation of costs and rewards on criminal behaviour.

Unlike social learning and strain theories, *social control theories* do not assume that the motivations to engage in criminal behaviour are derived from criminal learning or reinforcement schedules, or from stressful personal experiences. On the contrary, motivations for crime and other forms of antisocial behaviour are assumed to be part of human nature; everyone would engage in acts of force or fraud if they were free to do so. From the vantage point of social control theory, then, the key question is not why some persons commit crime, but why the rest of us do not. In the most influential of social control theories, Hirschi's (1969) theory of social bonds, natural inclinations to misbehave are restrained by the individual's social ties or bonds with conventional society. Individuals break the rules when the bonds that attach them to others, commit them to conventional lines of action, involve them in conventional activities, and sustain their belief in the rules themselves weaken or break. As individuals' social bonds drop away, in essence they are free to do as they please (Messner and Rosenfeld, 2007a: 53).[4]

Hirschi's social control theory is highly compatible with rational-choice perspectives on criminal behaviour. Individuals will engage in crime when it suits their interests and will refrain from crime when it does not. The rational actor will consider the rewards of crime in relation to the costs of displeasing those whose opinions he or she cares about, the risks to his or her conventional pursuits, the time and energy required, and whatever 'psychic' costs are associated with violating rules in which he or she believes.

---

[4] Strong social controls do not inevitably prevent or reduce criminal or deviant behaviour; sometimes they cause it. Consider Milgram's (1974) famous experiments on obedience to authority. By establishing strong social bonds between research subjects and the experimenter in the laboratory, Milgram was able to get large numbers of his subjects to administer what they thought were painful electric shocks to a 'victim.' They did so, according to Milgram, not because they derived pleasure from inflicting pain on another person, but because they wanted to conform to the experimenter's expectations.

The final social psychological perspective we take up in this chapter is Wikström's (2006, 2010) *situational-action theory*. Like Agnew's general strain theory, situational-action theory departs substantially from theories of rational choice in the explanation of criminal behaviour. Unlike general strain theory, however, situational-action theory does not emphasize the role of emotions in criminality; it focuses on morality.

The explanandum of SAT is the individual's decision to engage in criminal behaviour and, by extension, behaviour that violates moral rules more generally. The theory assumes that persons differ in their criminal propensity and their exposure to criminogenic settings. Criminal propensity is defined as the joint likelihood that an individual perceives a criminal act as an action alternative and chooses to carry out the act in a particular setting. A setting is defined as the portion or aspect of the environment (persons, objects, events) to which the individual is directly exposed and reacts. If criminal propensity is strong and exposure to criminogenic settings is frequent, the individual is likely to engage in crime. In the absence of these conditions, criminal behaviour is unlikely.

The two personal attributes that are most relevant to criminal behaviour are the individual's personal morality (adherence to moral rules) and his or her capacity for self-control. In somewhat parallel fashion, the features of the setting that are most relevant to criminal behaviour are its shared moral rules and deterrence properties (behavioural monitoring, intervention risk, and sanctions for rule violation). Importantly, self-control and deterrence guide criminal choices only when the individual's personal morality diverges from the moral rules of the setting. When the moral rules of the person and setting correspond with one another – when both either encourage or discourage criminal behaviour – the choice, in effect, is made and there is nothing to control or deter.

Wikström's theory, therefore, does not deny the role of choice in criminal behaviour, but the individual's decision to commit or refrain from crime depends on his or her personal morality and the moral rules that inhere in settings and not, in the first instance, on the rational calculation of costs and rewards. Moral norms condition the effect of cost–benefit calculations on criminal choices. Situational-action theory also incorporates the capacity of the individual to exert self-control, but self-control matters only when the individual must choose between actions that are consistent with his or her personal morality and those in keeping with the moral rules of the setting. If personal and setting rules are aligned, the individual's capacity for self-control does not matter because there is no choice to be made.

A final salient dimension of situational-action theory concerns the distinction between direct causes and indirect causes of criminal behaviour. Wikström (2006, 2010) characterizes the latter as the 'causes of the causes'. Criminal propensity, exposure to criminogenic settings, self-control and deterrence are direct causes of crime in the sense that, other things being equal, changes in one of these elements will produce changes in criminal behaviour. Because the theory's main objective is to explain the behaviour of individuals within settings, it devotes less attention to the features of social systems or personal development that explain variation in personal morality, in the moral rules of settings, and in individual exposure to more or less criminogenic settings. Nonetheless, the so-called causes of the causes have an important role in the theory because they help to explain the origins and development of personal morality and self-control, differences across settings in the moral rules and deterrence effectiveness, and the processes of social and self-selection that determine the variable exposure of individuals to settings of different kinds. This important, if underdeveloped, aspect of the theory provides a useful transition to our discussion of community-level theories of crime. Before we address the community-level theories, however, it is necessary to bring the economy back in to our discussion of criminal decision-making.

Criminal motivations, controls, opportunities, and the economy

As our summary of individual-level economic and criminological perspectives should make abundantly clear, the connection between economic conditions and the decision to engage in crime is very unlikely to be direct or unmediated. Yes, individuals seek to satisfy or maximize their interests. And, yes, this process usually entails some calculation of costs and rewards, and most people consider economic rewards to be important, especially in market capitalist societies. But the lesson to be drawn from the broad literature on criminological theory is that rational choice does not operate in a vacuum. It is bounded and conditioned, depending on the perspective, by biological traits, social learning, social bonds, emotions, self-control, and/or the interplay of personal and social moral rules.

If that were not enough, recall from Figure 2.1 that the motivations, controls, and opportunities specified in the individual-level theories mediate the relationship between economic conditions and crime in a two-step process. First, it must be established that specified economic conditions influence motivations, controls, and opportunities. Then, a relationship between crime and one or more of the mediating factors must be demonstrated. *Both* conditions must hold if we are to conclude that the economy has an indirect effect on crime. Most of the research conducted on the individual-level perspectives we have reviewed is limited to the second step of the mediating process, and few studies have evaluated the effects of all three of the mediating factors (for exceptions, see Agnew, 2006; Elliott et al., 1985). Moreover, the same economic conditions may have countervailing effects on crime if, for example, they strengthen criminal motivations while reducing criminal opportunities.

Where, then, does all of this leave economic conditions in the explanation of individual criminal behaviour? Several of the dominant individual-level perspectives in criminology provide a rationale for regarding low socioeconomic status as a *potential* risk factor for criminal behaviour. The underlying processes differ according to the theoretical approach, however, and in some of the theories, economic factors are either neglected or rejected as causes of crime.

In economic theories, the economy has a largely direct role in motivating rational criminal choices. Low socioeconomic status implies relatively meagre benefits of conformity relative to crime. Further, if it is assumed that the unemployed or low earners have 'less to lose' from legal punishment, they may perceive criminal behaviour to be less costly than do those of higher status. By contrast, the other individual-level perspectives relegate the economy, using Wikström's terminology, to the realm of the causes of the causes. As social-psychological theories, these perspectives seek to explain individual behaviour with reference to the proximate settings and circumstances that motivate, control, or provide opportunities for crime. Although they devote less attention to more distant or indirect causes, including the nature or functioning of the economy, several of the theories point to possible mechanisms that mediate the effect of socioeconomic status on criminal behaviour.

To illustrate, contemporary biosocial theories maintain that features of the individual's biological make-up, such as neuropsychological deficits, can interact with adverse social conditions to increase the likelihood of aggressive, antisocial, and criminal behaviour (Beaver, 2009; Fishbein, 2001). The development of such deficits in turn depends on a host of external factors, including the prenatal environment. It seems quite reasonable to hypothesize that low economic status tends to be associated with relatively poor maternal nutrition, which would increase the likelihood of impaired neurological development in the mother's offspring. The functioning of the economy would thus contribute to the 'production' of individuals whose biological constitutions make them particularly vulnerable to crime. In this scenario, the impact of economic conditions on crime is manifested a fairly long way down the causal chain.

Low socioeconomic status can also influence criminal learning, according to Akers (1998). Supportive evidence comes from Heimer's (1990) study of violent delinquency in a US national sample of males. Drawing on social learning theory, Heimer hypothesized that violent delinquents are more likely than other boys to have learned definitions favourable to violence and that the acquisition of violent conduct codes mediates the relationship between the boys' socioeconomic status and violent behaviour. Her study provides support for both hypotheses.

General strain theory also points to the possibility of a causal connection between economic conditions and crime. Limited access to economic resources is likely to create a perceived discrepancy between individuals' aspirations for social rewards and their expectations that they will actually obtain the rewards. This disjuncture between aspirations and expectations is a potential source of strain that can activate the negative emotional states that are identified by the theory as the proximate causes of crime. An experimental study by Rebellon et al. (2009) found evidence for these theoretical predictions. Subjects were randomly assigned to experimental conditions of high and low strain depending on the degree of discrepancy between expected and actual economic outcomes and 'fair' and actual economic outcomes. Those placed in the high-discrepancy/high-strain conditions displayed greater situational anger and reported a greater willingness to engage in theft than did subjects assigned to the low-discrepancy/low-strain conditions.

Economic conditions can also be linked with crime via social bonding theory. The processes that underlie these linkages vary depending on the element of the social bond under consideration. For one element of the bond – commitment – the logic of the argument closely resembles that of rational-choice approaches. Commitment refers to the accumulated investments in conformity that are advantageous to the individual. According to bonding theory, such commitments restrain people from indulging in their natural inclinations to misbehave because they do not want to jeopardize these investments. The restraining power of such commitments is likely to vary directly with levels of resources, implying that the economically deprived will be less securely bonded to the conventional order and thus be at comparatively high risk of criminal offending.

The element of the social bond that Hirschi (1969) termed 'attachment' has also been related to criminal and delinquent behaviour via family dynamics. Criminological theory and research indicate that parents with low socioeconomic status are less likely to employ the types of child-rearing techniques that foster close attachments with their children. Such attachments, in turn, are theorized to serve as key inhibitors of misbehaviour. Empirical research has supported these theoretical claims. As reported in a well-known study of the family context of juvenile delinquency by Sampson and Laub (1993: 64–98), an indicator of family socioeconomic status is positively related to a measure of attachment to parents, which in turn exhibits the expected negative association with both official and unofficial indicators of delinquency.

A connection between economic conditions and crime can also be hypothesized with reference to situational-action theory (SAT), although as the principal proponent of this theory acknowledges, the explication of the 'causes of the causes' of crime in SAT 'is very much a work still in progress' (Wikström, 2011: 68). Perhaps the most obvious linkage involves the various consequences of meagre economic resources for socialization, as noted above. According to SAT, a critical element in the perception-choice process underlying crime is the criminal propensity of the actor, which depends in turn on that person's commitment to conventional morality, cognitive development, and associated capacity to exercise self-control. Theory and research indicate that parents with low socioeconomic status are less likely to employ the kinds of child-rearing techniques that facilitate effective socialization. It follows that children from disadvantaged backgrounds are more likely to develop the criminal propensities that lead to criminal behaviour when they encounter settings conducive to crime.

In contrast with most criminological theories, self-control theory largely dismisses the role of economic factors in crime, except insofar as they influence the stock and flow of criminal opportunities (Gottfredson and Hirschi, 1990). If anything, the theory predicts that low self-control is a cause, not a consequence, of low socioeconomic status. Impulsive individuals who are incapable of developing strong attachments to others and think only of the 'here and now' are unlikely to devote the time and effort needed to do well in school and secure a good job and income. Any association between indicators of economic status and criminal behaviour thus simply reflects the effects of low self-control on both.

In summary, there are plentiful, if not universal, theoretical grounds for anticipating some type of causal relationship between economic conditions, specifically low socioeconomic status, and crime at the individual level.[5] There is also some evidence in the literature to support such a relationship, but the relationship appears to be less strong and robust than expected given the prima facie theoretical case for a connection (see Dunaway et al., 2000; Tittle et al., 1978). But upon reflection that should come as little surprise, because the theoretical literature depicts complex causal processes according to which the effect of economic conditions is likely to be indirect and contingent on a host of other characteristics of individuals and the immediate social settings within which they make choices and act. Finally, a significant

---

[5] What constitutes 'low' socioeconomic status varies historically and across societies that differ in economic development. Like most analysts, we conceive of low socioeconomic status in relative terms, that is, with reference to average or prevailing living standards in a given society at a particular point in history (cf. Wilkinson and Pickett, 2009).

limitation of these theories is that their focus is restricted for the most part to the individual level of analysis. A more complete explanation requires consideration of the larger social context.

As we shall see, economic conditions, especially economic deprivation or disadvantage, play a more central role in community-level perspectives on crime. And the empirical research at the community level tells a more consistent story about the impact of economic conditions on crime. But individual-level theories are implicated, if only implicitly, in these perspectives as well. Embedded in each of the community-level perspectives we review – routine activity, social disorganization, and subcultural theory – are assumptions about the nature of criminal decision-making. These assumptions retreat to the background, however, as our attention now moves from individual differences in criminal behaviour to the economic and social sources of variation in community crime rates.

Community-level mechanisms: routine activities, social disorganization and violent subcultures

Several decades ago, Tittle et al. (1978) published a provocative review of the literature on the relationship between social class and crime/delinquency. The main conclusion of their analysis was stated succinctly and unambiguously in the first part of the title of their article: 'The Myth of Social Class and Criminality'. In response to this study, the criminologist John Braithwaite had this to say: 'Perhaps Tittle et al. take their own findings seriously and adopt no extra precautions when moving about in the slums of the world's great cities than they do when walking in the middle class areas of such cities' (1981: 37).

Braithwaite's remark, although somewhat tongue-in-cheek, underscores an important result in reviews of the relationship between crime and socioeconomic status. Studies of individual criminal behaviour generally find a weak relationship, whereas community-level studies consistently report that crime rates are higher in economically disadvantaged neighbourhoods than in middle-class neighbourhoods. In fact, a recent systematic review concluded that the socioeconomic status of a group or community is the single strongest predictor of crime at the macro level (Pratt and Cullen, 2005). We do not attempt to resolve the discrepancy between the findings of micro- and macro-level research on the relationship between crime and socioeconomic status. We focus instead on the theoretical mechanisms that link crime and socioeconomic status at the community level.

What then are the broader features of communities that help to explain why some communities have higher crime rates than others? How do those conditions mediate the relationship between economic conditions and crime? Three community-level criminological perspectives directly confront these questions: the *routine activities* perspective (Cohen and Felson, 1979; Felson, 2002); the classical *social disorganization* arguments of the early Chicago School theorists (Shaw and McKay, 1969), and recent refinements of classical disorganization theory in the *systemic model of community control* (Bursik and Grasmick, 1993) and the theory of *collective efficacy* (Sampson et al., 1997); and the *subcultural* perspective, especially as applied in Anderson's (1999) study of the 'code of the street'. The common and defining feature of each of these theoretical traditions is their contention that the impact of economic disadvantage on community crime rates is largely indirect. Poverty and unemployment influence crime rates, depending on the perspective, by altering the routine activities of everyday life, increasing social disorganization and reducing social control, or facilitating the development of violent conduct codes.

Routine activities and criminal opportunity

Routine-activities theory represents an important breakthrough in the explanation of crime by directing attention to the opportunities for crime and away from the criminal propensities of would-be offenders. Criminology had been dominated by theories and research on criminal propensities, including the motivations, incentives, pressures and controls that influence decision-making. Too little attention was devoted to the requirements of crime itself, that is, the conditions that must exist for crime of a given type to occur. By shifting the emphasis to the characteristics of settings and, importantly, crime targets or victims that increase or reduce criminal opportunities, the routine-activities theorists have helped to correct a significant imbalance of emphasis in the study of crime.[6]

The routine-activities perspective, first introduced by Cohen and Felson (1979), holds that three essential conditions must exist for crime to occur: (1) proximity to motivated offenders; (2) the presence of suitable targets; and (3) the absence of capable guardians. If one of these conditions is lacking, crime will not take place. Other than the reference to motivated offenders, the theory has little to say about criminal decision-making per se. Even so, routine-activities theory rests squarely in the rational-choice tradition. Whatever else may motivate them to engage in crime, offenders size up the opportunities for crime by assessing the suitability or attractiveness of a potential target against the chances of detection by a capable guardian (for examples, see Wright and Decker, 1997).

The suitability of a crime target is determined by its value to the offender (diamonds are worth more than costume jewellery), its portability (laptops are easier to carry away than desk-top computers), and ease of access to and egress from the crime scene (suicide terrorism eliminates the egress problem). Guardianship comes in many forms, animate and inanimate, including guard dogs, night watchmen, police officers, onlookers, surveillance cameras, and burglar alarms. Although it has been applied primarily to property crimes, routine-activities theory has also been used to explain violent offending (see Felson, 2002).

Routine-activities theorists and researchers do not dwell on the relationship between crime and the socioeconomic composition of a community. Yet hiring security guards and installing surveillance cameras and alarms are expensive forms of guardianship, and they are more likely to be found in affluent communities than in poor ones. The ultimate form of residential protection is the so-called gated community that keeps outsiders at bay with physical barriers, guard posts, and strict

---

[6] A close theoretical cousin to the routine-activities perspective is the *lifestyle* theory of crime, developed by Michael Hindelang and colleagues (Hindelang et al., 1978). Lifestyle theory seeks to explain variation in criminal victimization in terms of the activity patterns of crime victims. We subsume the insights of lifestyle theory in our discussion of the routine-activities perspective.

rules of access (Blakely and Snyder, 1998). Very few gated communities are located in low-income neighbourhoods.

To the extent it is effective, heightened guardianship helps to explain why crime rates are typically lower in high-income neighbourhoods. On the other hand, affluent areas are more apt to contain items of value to offenders, such as luxury automobiles and expensive electronic goods. In short, there is more worth stealing in well-off neighbourhoods. That is why the residents of these areas go to such lengths to guard against crime.

But affluent neighbourhoods do not have a monopoly on the means of guardianship. Even casual observation of disadvantaged communities yields plentiful evidence of security guards, 'burglar bars' on doors and windows, shopkeepers separated from customers by thick plate glass, and fortress-like housing projects. The reasons for enhanced guardianship, however, differ in poor and affluent neighbourhoods. Affluent neighbourhoods seek to reduce criminal opportunities because of the attractiveness of their crime targets; many poor neighbourhoods seek to enhance guardianship due to their proximity to motivated offenders.

The move away from offender-based explanations of crime is both a weakness and a strength of routine-activities theory. Offender 'motivation', viewed broadly as those individual and social characteristics that contribute to criminal propensities, clearly matters in the study of crime. Moreover, criminal motivations and opportunities can have contrasting effects on crime commission. The very conditions, including economic change, that strengthen the motivation to commit crime may also reduce criminal opportunities. A good example is change in the unemployment rate.

When the unemployment rate rises, the motivation to engage in criminal behaviour may increase, as growing numbers of persons suffer losses in legitimate income. But increasing unemployment also means that more people remain at home, when they would otherwise have been at work, and act as guardians of their own households and perhaps of other homes in the neighbourhood. Burglars wish to avoid detection and therefore prefer unoccupied over occupied targets or those that are within view of the neighbours (Wright and Decker, 1994). The enhanced guardianship that accompanies increased unemployment thereby reduces the opportunity for residential burglary.

If the same economic conditions strengthen criminal motivations and reduce criminal opportunities, studies that fail to distinguish these countervailing effects from one another may incorrectly conclude that economic change has little or no effect on crime. This is the scenario depicted in Panel C of Figure 1.2 in the previous chapter in which the relationship between crime and the economy is mediated by two variables that operate in countervailing ways. In the unemployment example, rising joblessness has a positive 'motivation effect' and a negative 'opportunity effect' on residential burglary (cf. Cantor and Land, 1985).

A comprehensive explanation of the effect of economic conditions on crime must take into account both the effect on criminal opportunities, the focus of the routine-activities perspective, and the effect on criminal propensities, the traditional centre of attention in criminological theory. We now shift focus to perspectives that emphasize the social and cultural characteristics of communities that affect the propensity to engage in crime.

Community disorganization and social control

At the beginning of the twentieth century, the city of Chicago was home to about 1.7 million people. Chicago's population grew to just under 2.2 million in 1910, 2.7 million in 1920, and reached nearly 3.4 million by 1930, roughly doubling in size in just three decades.[7] During this period, Chicago's population growth resulted mainly from the migration to the city of immigrants from Southern and Eastern Europe and of African-Americans and whites from the American South. By and large, the newcomers were unskilled workers of very modest means. They joined previous migrants from Northern Europe who had settled in the city's neighbourhoods during the nineteenth century.

The changing ethnic and socioeconomic composition of Chicago's population caught the attention of the newly formed sociology department at the University of Chicago. What came to be called the 'Chicago

---

[7] The population figures were compiled by Dennis McClendon at http://tigger.uic.edu/depts/ahaa/imagebase/chimaps/mcclendon.html. Accessed 17 May 2011.

School' of urban sociology conducted research and developed new theories to explain the cultural and social changes that were dramatically transforming the city's neighbourhoods and the social problems, including crime, which accompanied those changes. To this day, Chicago remains the epicentre of much research on urban crime, and the Chicago School's theoretical contributions remain the most influential perspectives for understanding the connection between communities and crime (see Sampson, 2002).

Two members of the early Chicago School, Clifford Shaw and Henry D. McKay, made a fascinating observation about crime in Chicago's neighbourhoods in the early part of the twentieth century. Even as the ethnic composition of a neighbourhood changed, rates of crime and delinquency remained fairly stable. High crime rates persisted in neighbourhoods located close to the city's centre and crime rates remained low in outlying areas, regardless of who lived there. Shaw and McKay (1969) reasoned that there must be something about a neighbourhood itself, apart from the ethnic or national origin of its residents, that explains the stubborn persistence of crime in some places and the rarity of crime in others. On the basis of statistics on court referrals of delinquents and neighbourhood surveys, they concluded that a neighbourhood's level of delinquency and crime reflects its degree of *social disorganization*, which they defined as the capacity of residents to realize common values and goals. Organized communities typically enjoy low levels of crime. Disorganized communities suffer from high crime rates, not because their residents are indifferent to crime or desire it, but because they are incapable of controlling it. The failure to achieve low crime rates, a common goal of nearly all city residents, results then from weak or ineffective *social controls*. Effective social control, according to Shaw and McKay (1969), is the hallmark of neighbourhood social organization.

If crime in disorganized neighbourhoods results from weak or ineffective social controls, what aspects of the neighbourhood context prevent residents from developing or applying effective social controls? Shaw and McKay (1969) identified three characteristics of communities that impede their capacity to control crime: economic deprivation, residential instability, and population heterogeneity. They found a strong negative correlation between the crime rates and socioeconomic composition of Chicago neighbourhoods: the lower the economic status of the neighbourhood, the higher the crime rate. Areas with limited economic resources cannot develop or sustain the youth organizations, community centres, athletic leagues, libraries, and other neighbourhood amenities that attach youth to conventional adult role models, supervise their day-to-day activities, provide legitimate means of achievement and status, and thereby control delinquency and crime. Families of limited means, in which both parents work long hours away from home, often cannot adequately monitor the comings and goings of children and adolescents. In these and other ways, impoverished communities are unable to build up the family and community controls that limit delinquent and criminal activity.

Another source of weak social control, according to Shaw and McKay (1969), is residential instability. They and other early Chicago School researchers referred to neighbourhoods with persistently high crime rates as 'zones in transition', meaning that their populations are subject to rapid and continuous turnover as families move in, stay for a brief period, and then move out. Strong attachments to the community are difficult to sustain under such conditions, especially when many residents assume that they or their neighbours will not remain in the area for long. Weak or transitory community attachments impede the ability of residents to control delinquency and crime.

Finally, Shaw and McKay (1969) argued that population heterogeneity, or differences in language, ethnicity and religion among community members, make it difficult for residents to communicate with one another and may trigger mistrust and tensions across group lines. These conditions, they held, also weaken community controls and increase crime.

We have suggested that the community-level perspectives draw explicitly or implicitly on theories of individual criminal behaviour. As we have seen, the routine-activities perspective presupposes that individuals are rational actors who weigh the costs and benefits of available opportunities for crime. Although it was developed many years later, social-control theory supplies the individual-level assumptions that are most compatible with Shaw and McKay's disorganization perspective on community crime rates. Both theories assume that crime varies inversely with the strength of social controls. The disorganized community is one in which individuals' attachments to one another (parent to child, neighbour to neighbour) are fleeting and commitments to and involvement in conventional activities are weak.

One significant difference in emphasis between Shaw and McKay's disorganization theory and Hirschi's theory of social bonds concerns the bonding element that Hirschi termed 'belief'. Hirschi (1969) assumed that delinquency and crime vary with the strength of an individual's belief in conventional norms and values. The stronger their belief in the conventional moral order, other things being equal, the lower the probability that individuals will engage in delinquent or criminal behaviour. Hirschi argued against the idea that delinquent behaviour reflects or is sustained by a separate system of 'delinquent' norms and values. Shaw and McKay (1969), by contrast, proposed that a delinquent subculture – attitudes and beliefs that promote delinquent behaviour – does develop in disorganized communities. The durability of the delinquent value system, they held, is an important reason why delinquent and criminal behaviour persists in areas characterized by rapid population turnover, as new arrivals are socialized in the deviant conduct codes of former inhabitants. In a real sense, the delinquent subculture stays in the neighbourhood, even as residents come and go.

The disorganization perspective on community crime rates fell into disfavour among sociologists and criminologists during the post-World War II period. The concept of the 'disorganized' community was attacked by Chicago-School insiders, notably Edwin Sutherland (1986), who objected to the pejorative implications of the depiction of impoverished and unstable communities as incapable of controlling themselves and proposed the alternative conception of 'differential social organization' (see Messner and Rosenfeld, 2007a: 56–7). Outsiders equated the concept of disorganization with the 'pathological' tradition in sociology that faulted the urban poor for diverging from small-town, Protestant, middle-class standards of decency (Mills, 1943). In the 1980s, however, disorganization theory experienced a comeback, in part due to its compatibility with Hirschi's social control theory, which was enormously popular during that period. The renewed respectability of disorganization theory was also inspired by the increased attention devoted to it by researchers in the Chicago-School tradition who were rediscovering the role of community dynamics in the production and control of crime (Bursik, 1988; Sampson and Groves, 1989; Stark, 1987).

As social disorganization was put back in the theoretical toolkit of criminology, it was scrubbed clean of the pejorative connotations that had disturbed earlier critics (Bursik, 1988) and elaborated and revised to account for changes in the community dynamics of the contemporary city. Bursik and Grasmick (1993) elaborated on the types of social control that account for the variation in crime rates across urban neighbourhoods. Community controls, they argued, come in three primary forms: private, parochial and public. Private controls emanate from the intimate interactions of parents and children, friends and neighbours. Parochial controls reside in the secondary associations of the community, including local businesses, schools, churches, clubs, community organizations and recreation centres. Public controls inhere in the relationship between the local community and centres of power and influence in the city. The three forms of community control, according to Bursik and Grasmick (1993), are grounded in relational networks and operate in a 'systemic' fashion, each nourished by the others. The maintenance of vibrant and effective private and parochial controls, in particular, depends on the strength of a community's public controls.

Although they did not stress the distinction between them, Shaw and McKay (1969) focused on the importance of private and parochial social controls, but they largely neglected public controls in their research on the social sources of delinquency and crime in Chicago. Yet, the position of a community in the political economy of the city – a neighbourhood's 'clout' with city hall – is a critical component of its capacity to control its borders and attract essential city services such as trash collection, street maintenance, enforcement of building codes, and vigilant and fair policing. Communities with weak public controls will have difficulty sustaining private and parochial controls and are vulnerable to criminal activity from local residents and outsiders alike.

A second significant theoretical innovation in the social-disorganization framework is Sampson and colleagues' formulation of the concept of collective efficacy. Sampson et al. (1997) defined collective efficacy in terms of two dimensions: a community's capacity for collective action and residents' willingness to take action to maintain order and control. They argued that the capacity for collective action, as indicated, for example, by informal ties among residents and membership in community organizations, is by itself not sufficient to control disorder and crime. Residents must also be willing to actively intervene in the public life of the community, for example, by monitoring the behaviour of adolescents on the street and reporting misbehaviour to their parents. In a study of Chicago neighbourhoods, Sampson et al. (1997) found that a measure of collective efficacy was inversely related to multiple indicators of neighbourhood violence and mediated the effects on these indicators of neighbourhood economic disadvantage and residential instability.

In recent years, researchers have continued to test and refine the disorganization perspective with new data, research designs, measurement strategies, and theoretical constructs (see Kubrin and Weitzer, 2003). One important development is the use of spatial data analysis methods to assess the effects of crime and its causes in a community on adjacent areas (e.g., Messner et al., 1999; Morenoff et al., 2001; Rosenfeld et al., 1999). Another is mounting research on the *reciprocal* effects of community disorganization and crime (see Kubrin and Weitzer, 2003: 389–91; Sampson, 2006: 157–9). Just as economic deprivation and residential instability may increase the level of crime in a community, crime itself is a source of disorganization to the degree that it increases poverty and instability, as better-off residents move out of areas where crime rates are high or increasing.

Finally, the walls separating the disorganization perspective and subcultural theories of crime and delinquency have begun to come down. Hirschi's (1969) and Kornhauser's (1978) once prominent contention concerning the relationship between subculture and crime that 'never the twain shall meet' has given way to a renewed appreciation for the ways in which disadvantaged social circumstances can give rise to attitudes and beliefs that facilitate crime, especially criminal violence. Perhaps no recent work has had a greater influence on the resurgence of subcultural theories of crime than Elijah Anderson's *Code of the Street*.

Bringing culture back in: violence and the code of the street

Anderson's (1999) account of violence in inner-city Philadelphia is anchored in a theoretical framework that stresses the debilitating effects of long-term joblessness, community instability, and alienation from formal authority, especially the police, among the urban poor. But Anderson's study does not stop there. Conditions of chronic deprivation, isolation, and alienation give rise to more or less distinctive cultural orientations in a segment of the urban underclass, according to Anderson, that promote violent responses to perceived insults and threats. Once acquired, these violent conduct norms are hard to shake, even in settings where they are not needed and may be counterproductive (e.g., at school and work). Although borne of economic hardship and racial exclusion, the 'code of the street' takes on a life of its own, and inhabitants of the communities where it prevails had better learn its dos and don'ts or risk becoming prey to those who live by the code.

A key question in Anderson's (1999) ethnographic description of the origins and functions of the code of the street is whether such 'oppositional cultures', as they have been termed, increase or reduce the risk of victimization among adherents. On the one hand, knowing the code would seem to be a necessity for staying alive and healthy in an environment where the threat of violence is ever present. On the other hand, however, the code explicitly endorses and encourages violence in response to threats from others and therefore likely amplifies the level of violence in those communities where many young men adopt it, even if for defensive purposes. A study of African-American adolescents found that those who adhere to the tenets of the code of the street have higher rates of victimization than adolescents who reject the code (Stewart et al., 2006). But even if adopting the code reduces the risk of personal victimization, violent conduct norms may still contribute to the overall level of violence in places where they are widespread by encouraging violent retaliation to threats, slights, insults, and 'disrespect' (see Jacobs and Wright, 2006).

Anderson's (1999) conception of the code of the street fits within the broader tradition of social-learning theories of deviant and criminal behaviour. The analogue of the social-learning perspective at the community level of analysis is *cultural deviance theory* (Messner and Rosenfeld, 2007a: 51–3).[8] Cultural deviance theory holds that subcultures consisting

---

[8] We characterize cultural deviance theory as an analogue at the community level of social learning theory, but we do not claim that the two are equivalent. Social learning theory incorporates non-cultural as well as cultural learning mechanisms, and it allows for structural as well as cultural determinants of human behaviour. See Akers and Jensen (2006).

of conduct norms that conflict with those of the dominant culture, encourage deviant and criminal behaviour. Continuing debate in the social sciences concerns the degree to which deviant subcultures arise in response to structural conditions, such as economic deprivation and racial discrimination, and disappear with changes in those conditions. The question, in other words, is whether a deviant subculture, such as the code of the street, constitutes an adaptation to structural disadvantages that prevent group members from realizing the values and goals of the dominant culture, or whether such subcultures are free-standing normative systems, transmitted from one generation to the next, that persist over time even as the structural circumstances of the group are altered.

A strong statement of the 'free-standing' view of deviant subcultures is Walter Miller's (1958) theory of lower-class culture. Miller argued that the 'focal concerns' of lower-class culture, including an emphasis on trouble, toughness, and excitement, are not responses to the inability of members of the lower class to achieve middle-class respectability and success. Rather, lower-class culture is an independent normative system that promotes criminal and violent behaviour quite apart from the structural or material disadvantages of lower-class life (see also Wolfgang and Ferracuti, 1967).[9]

The strong version of the cultural-deviance perspective came under criticism shortly after Miller (1958) published his original argument (e.g., Rainwater, 1970; Rodman, 1963), and is far from the consensus view in contemporary criminology. It certainly does not jibe with Anderson's (1999) explanation of the origins of the code of the street, which he viewed as a cultural adaptation to the disadvantaged circumstances of inner-city communities. As noted above, social-disorganization theorists and researchers in the Chicago-School tradition have also developed a renewed appreciation for the role of more or less distinctive cultural norms in the production of crime and violence. But the new conceptions of culture are a far cry from Miller's (1958) view of lower-class focal concerns as essentially unrelated to structural disadvantage (see, for example, Sampson and Bean, 2006).

---

[9] The independence from middle-class standards of Miller's (1958) lower-class focal concerns is a matter of debate. Matza and Sykes (1961) pointed out that the emphasis on toughness and excitement, for example, is actually quite widespread, especially among adolescents in contemporary societies.

* * *

It has become fashionable in the popular media and some criminological circles to declare that, like politics, 'all crime is local'. In fact, some criminologists argue that the 'street segment' is the most appropriate unit of analysis for the study of crime in communities, given the pronounced variation in crime rates that can occur within census tracts or neighbourhoods (e.g., Eck and Weisburd, 1995; Weisburd and Bruinsma, 2009). Although it is true that criminal acts occur at specific points in time and space and may vary in frequency across places within the same neighbourhood, that tells us that crime is *manifested* in small social spaces and not necessarily that its *causes* are similarly circumscribed. As with politics and crime, we might say that all unemployment or heart disease is local, but it would be unwise to limit the search for the causes of unemployment and heart disease to the local communities, much less the specific addresses, where they occur. Our investigation of the economic causes of crime should also extend beyond the confines of the immediate social surround and encompass the institutional forces that affect local crime rates. William Julius Wilson's groundbreaking explanation of the transformation of inner-city neighbourhoods in the United States after World War II is a fitting point of departure.

Economic transformation, community disadvantage, and crime

Each of the community-level perspectives we have reviewed carves out a large space for the economy as an indirect cause of crime. The routine-activities perspective emphasizes the role of the economy in structuring criminal opportunities. The disorganization and subcultural perspectives devote greater attention to how economic conditions influence criminal propensities, by weakening community social controls, spawning subcultures that promote or tolerate criminal activity, or both. The three approaches share a common emphasis on conditions within the local community (or city) that lead to high or low rates of crime. Even though they are typically based on studies of a single locality, however, the community-level perspectives aspire to generality.

Disorganization or violent conduct norms do not generate crime in Chicago or Philadelphia alone. As scientific theories, the community perspectives seek to explain crime wherever the relevant conditions are present. Yet, one gets little sense from these perspectives of how local communities are themselves shaped by broader societal and historical changes. Anderson (1999) does allude to society-wide economic and social changes that set the stage for the development of violent street codes in the inner city, but he does not trace the development of those changes in any detail. Wilson's work provides the details.

Wilson was in the sociology department at the University of Chicago when he published his landmark study, *The Truly Disadvantaged* (Wilson, 1987). Like the early twentieth-century Chicago-School theorists and researchers before him, Wilson conducted his research in the context of demographic upheavals that were transforming the social landscape of Chicago. Between 1940 and 1970, Chicago's African-American population nearly quadrupled in size, from 278,000 to 1.1 million residents (Gibson and Jung, 2005). As with the first 'Great Migration' of black Southerners to Northern cities earlier in the century, the new arrivals hoped for more economic opportunities and less racial discrimination in the 'Promised Land' (Lemann, 1991). For a time, the hopes of many migrants were realized in Chicago's booming wartime and early post-war economy. But by the 1960s, black unemployment was on the rise, and Wilson (1987) noted the disturbing growth of what he termed 'concentrated disadvantage' in Chicago's African-American neighbourhoods. Chronically high levels of joblessness, poverty, and family disruption had taken hold in the inner city, along with soaring crime rates. What caused this reversal of fortune for Chicago's black population?

Wilson (1987) explained that the growth of concentrated disadvantage stemmed in part from the reduction of racial barriers to geographic mobility during the latter half of the twentieth century. As middle-class blacks took advantage of new housing opportunities, they moved out of neighbourhoods they had shared with low-income blacks, leaving behind an increasingly impoverished and socially isolated under-class population. But that was only part of the problem. What also had to be explained was the absolute growth in unemployment, especially among poorly educated black men. Why had so many simply given up looking for work and begun to seek their fortunes in the illicit economy of drugs and crime?

The sources of chronic joblessness were not to be found, according to Wilson, in the flawed characters of the urban poor or the growing divide between underclass and middle-class neighbourhoods. If anything, deficiencies in human capital and social isolation were the consequences, not the causes, of enduring unemployment. The ultimate causes were to be found in a qualitative shift in the structure of employment opportunities. Jobs in the manufacturing sector of the economy, that had once been filled by persons with little formal education, were disappearing. They were replaced by work, even in the growing service sector, that required a high-school education, at a minimum, and increasingly two or more years of college or advanced technical training. The decline of the manufacturing sector and the rise of the so-called post-industrial or 'information' economy left a large fraction of the urban poor without legitimate economic opportunities, removed the secure employment base that is essential for neighbourhood stability, led to family disruption as the number of 'marriageable' men diminished, and increased the crime rates of the neighbourhoods where these multiple disadvantages were concentrated.

These were 'neighbourhood' problems to be sure, but their origins lay far beyond the Chicago's South Side or city hall, for that matter. They resulted from structural changes in the economy that were nationwide – indeed, global – in scope and consequence. As such, their solution would require policies of comparable magnitude. Wilson (1987) called for massive job-creation programmes that would put the urban poor back to work. Nothing less would reverse the disastrous spiral of joblessness, concentrated neighbourhood disadvantage, and crime.

Although *The Truly Disadvantaged* met with almost universal acclaim, Wilson's (1987) argument was not without its critics. Some argued that the family and community disabilities that afflicted Chicago's underclass predated the second Great Migration and were imported from the South (Lemann, 1991). Others suggested that Wilson underestimated the continuing significance of racial discrimination in circumscribing the opportunities of both poor and middle-class African-Americans in the latter half of the twentieth century (Massey and Denton, 1993; see also Wilson, 1980). The latter critique merits extended discussion.

Wilson (1980, 1987) credited the civil-rights movement and equal-opportunity legislation as the impetus for the movement of middle-class

African-Americans away from the neighbourhoods they once cohabited with the poor. But he did not give sufficient emphasis, according to Massey and Denton (1993), to another demographic shift of even greater consequence for blacks in the urban North: white flight. As blacks moved into white neighbourhoods, more often than not the whites moved out – including out of the city. As mentioned, like the early Chicago-School sociologists, Wilson was struck by the huge influx of black migrants to Chicago, but the second Great Migration differed from the first in a decisive respect. The earlier in-migration of Europeans and African-Americans was accompanied by – indeed, was largely responsible for – enormous growth in the city's population. Exactly the reverse occurred in the decades after World War II. Chicago's population peaked in 1950, at 3.6 million inhabitants, and then fell steadily over the next half century (Gibson and Jung, 2005). The vast majority of those leaving the city for the suburbs were white.

The rapid suburbanization of the white population during the post-war period occurred for several reasons (see Boustan, 2010), but the effects on the central city are clear. The movement of hundreds of thousands of middle-class white families out of the city eroded the urban tax base, undermined public schools, depleted city services and amenities, and hastened the suburbanization of employment – all of which fell especially hard on the urban poor. It is difficult to deny the continuing centrality of race in the lives of the 'truly disadvantaged'.

If Wilson is rightly criticized for downplaying the significance of race in shaping the context of urban disadvantage, he cannot be faulted for missing the forest for the trees in his analysis of the economic sources of neighbourhood disorder and crime. Wilson's (1987) analysis falls within the social-disorganization tradition of the Chicago School, augmented by a theory of social change, the 'deindustrialization' thesis, that locates the ultimate causes of community disadvantage, disorder, and crime in the institutional transformation of the economy. The very rules of the economic game – leave school and find a union job in a mill or factory that pays enough to support a family – were upended in the final decades of the last century. This is not a story of cyclical economic change, the recurrent ups and downs of the economy resulting in temporary shifts in the unemployment rate, but of massive and long-lasting alterations in the structure of employment opportunities that change the very nature of work and produce new categories of economic winners and losers. This is a story of *institutional* change, and to understand such change and its consequences requires an institutional perspective. In the next chapter, we trace the intellectual history of an institutional perspective on the economy and crime.

THREE

bringing in institutions: markets, morality, and crime

The reliance on markets to structure the production and distribution of goods and services has become a taken-for-granted feature of modern life. Fundamentally different economic arrangements, such as the state socialism of the former Soviet Union and the centralized command economy of Maoist China, have been relegated to the dustbin of history. There is certainly variation in the forms of market capitalism observed throughout the globe, as well as lively political disagreements in many nations about the proper role of government intervention in a market economy. But questions about whether capitalist markets are desirable or viable are conspicuously absent from contemporary intellectual and political debate.

It turns out, however, that such questions inspired much of the theorizing of the classical figures in social thought. One position, which emerged from the liberal political philosophy and economic theory of the Enlightenment, envisions a social order in market-oriented societies that is characterized by mutually satisfying relationships centred on the voluntary exchange of goods and services. Involvement in the commercial transactions of the marketplace is seen as having a 'civilizing' influence on social conduct (Hirschman, 1992: 106–9). The opposite position, embraced by critics of capitalism, maintains that capitalist markets have a corrosive impact on social controls, which leads ultimately to disorder and moral decline. In this view, markets function at peak efficiency precisely to the extent that they free persons from the restraints on self-interested behaviour imposed by political, social, or moral obligations and ties. Although the contending sides in the 'markets and morality' debates arrive at very different, and at times diametrically opposed, assessments of the broader impacts of market capitalism, they all adopt distinctively institutional approaches to understanding the sources of social order and disorder. As such, they offer keen insights and a working model for the formulation of an institutional perspective in the study of crime.

In this chapter, we present an institutional analytic framework for explaining the level and types of crime found in societies of different types and the same society during different historical periods. Social institutions are defined; institutions are distinguished from their organizational manifestations with which they are commonly confused; and the structure, regulation, and performance of institutions in complex societies are highlighted. We then introduce institutional-anomie theory as one attempt to link social institutions to crime and, specifically, to shed light on the relationship between crime and the institutional structure of the economy. The chapter concludes by summarizing the contribution of institutional analysis to criminological theory, which anticipates the empirical research on the economy and crime discussed in Chapter 4.

Social institutions

An exciting development in criminological theory over the course of the past few decades has been the renewed attention devoted to the role of social institutions, a development that Karstedt (2010) has aptly labelled the 'new institutionalism'. This new institutionalism has been manifested most prominently in recent research on criminal punishment. In a series of illuminating studies, scholars have described the ways in which the societal response to criminal offending reflects the broader complex of social institutions and also the ways in which punishment regimes themselves affect other components of the institutional order (Cavadino and Dignan, 2006; Garland, 1990, 2001, 2010; Gottschalk, 2006; Lacey, 2008; Simon, 1993; Western, 2006).

Recognition of the centrality of institutions to an understanding of the societal response to crime is perhaps not surprising, given that what is commonly referred to as the 'criminal justice system' is itself an institution (or an institutional subsystem). As we have observed elsewhere, however, 'institutional analysis has been seriously underdeveloped in *etiological* analyses of crime...', that is, in explanations of the causes of crime (Messner and Rosenfeld, 2007b: 83). As shown in the previous chapter, the most influential etiological theories in contemporary criminology (such as rational choice, social control, social disorganization, self-control, strain, situational-action, and learning theories) locate the causes of crime in properties of individual actors, the interaction of individual actors and their immediate settings, or features of the localized neighbourhood. We find much merit in these efforts, but to our minds the associated explanations of the causes of crime are incomplete in a fundamental respect. They fail to take into account the profound ways in which individual action and the proximate settings for such action are constrained by, and are reflective of, the prevailing institutional order of a given society at a particular moment in time.

Our claim that criminologists have given insufficient attention to the role of social institutions in understanding the causes of crime might seem perplexing at first glance. After all, references to the potential influence of families, schools, and other features of the social context of individual behaviour abound in criminological theory and research, and these entities are often characterized as 'institutions'. But such usage confuses social institutions with their organizational manifestations. To avoid such confusion, it is important to define the concept of a social institution clearly and to situate this conceptualization within the context of a broader understanding of the macro-social organization of societal settings, or what has been called the *social system*.

Our conceptualization of social institutions draws heavily on the classic sociological theorizing of Talcott Parsons (1951, 1990 [1934]) and the influential work of the institutional economist Douglas North (1990). According to Parsons, the concept of a social institution refers to the *rules* that govern behaviour within a social system. Social systems, in turn, consist of more or less distinctive patterns of culture and social structure and their interrelations in society. Culture refers to the values, beliefs, and meanings that are shared by members of a society.

Social structure consists of the organizations, statuses, and roles through which culture is realized and enacted in everyday life. The institutional rules (often referred to as 'norms') are designed to bind culture and social structure into an ongoing social system.

In any given social system, numerous rules or norms apply to a diverse array of behaviours. It is thus useful to conceptualize the *subsystems* of norms that pertain to specified tasks that can be differentiated on the basis of the contributions that these tasks make to the functioning of society and its capacity to endure over time. These subsystems of regulatory norms constitute the major social institutions in a society as commonly understood (e.g., the economy, the polity, the family, religion). Douglas North (1990: 3) offers a compatible conceptualization of social institutions, describing them as the 'rules of the game' that guide human interaction.

Conceiving of social institutions as the normative rules of the game that facilitate the functioning of social systems carries several important implications concerning the phenomenon of crime. First, given the salience of social institutions in channelling social behaviour in general, the form and frequency of criminal behaviour are likely to be linked to the institutional order. As Durkheim (1966 [1895]: 70) observed, crime is a social fact 'bound up with the fundamental conditions of all social life'. Different social systems, and accordingly different institutional orders, should have characteristically distinct patterns and levels of crime. Moreover, patterns and levels of crime in any given social system are likely to vary across different historical periods, following the currents of social change, its impact on institutional settings, and the adaptive processes within the institutional order.

Second, if crime is fundamentally social in origin, level, and type, then crime is *normal* (Durkheim, 1966 [1895]). It is normal in the sense of being an expected outcome of the prevailing social organization. Every society thus has a normal rate of crime, that is, the crime rate generated by the prevailing institutional order. As societies undergo fundamental social transformations, the normal crime rate should therefore be 'reset', reflecting the newly emerging form of the institutional order.

Third, notwithstanding historical variability in levels and forms of crime in concrete societies, the crime rate can never be driven to zero.

This follows from the notion that crime is normal and 'bound up' with fundamental social conditions. Even if a particular type of crime is extinguished, another type will take its place. For example, violent crime rates have fallen in most Western societies since the late Middle Ages, but rates of property crime have risen over the same period (Eisner, 2001; Shelley, 1981). This reflects fundamental social changes (e.g., new modes of transportation and economic organization) that altered the rules of the game for violent behaviour and the ways in which modern societies organized social control, thus eliminating or reducing some types of crime and fostering the ascendancy of others.

Fourth, the social normality of crime implies that crime rates may fall *too low* for the effective operation of a society. This idea follows directly from the premise that crime is a characteristic feature of a society's institutional makeup. As Durkheim (1966 [1895]: 72) wrote: 'Crime ... must no longer be conceived as an evil that cannot be too much suppressed. There is no occasion for self-congratulation when the crime rate drops below the average level, for we may be certain that this apparent progress is associated with some social disorder.' As an example, consider the low rates of robbery, burglary, and other forms of street crime that prevailed in the former Soviet Union, simultaneously with high rates of corruption (Karstedt, 2003). A garrison state can suppress street crime, but at great social cost.

In short, from an institutional perspective, crime is a normal property of social systems which reflects the core features of the institutional order. Different institutional arrangements are expected to generate distinctive levels and types of crime, which should change along with alterations to these institutional arrangements. But how, specifically, should institutional analysis be carried out? What aspects of institutions are most relevant to criminological inquiry? How can they be deployed as analytical tools in empirical studies of crime?

Institutional analysis

The following three dimensions of social institutions are particularly important when analyzing the implications of the institutional order of societies for crime: institutional *structure*, institutional *regulation* and institutional *performance*. Institutional structure encompasses the specific content of the rules and their internal consistency and compatibility. Variation in the content of rules essentially involves qualitative comparisons. Different societies are likely to have different rules, and the nature of the rules in a given society inevitably changes over time. Consider, for example, the differences in the rules governing command and market economies. Market economies allocate resources on the basis of price. Command economies, by contrast, allocate resources according to centralized planning and control.

Internal consistency and compatibility can be conceptualized quantitatively. The consistency of the rules within a given institutional domain is in principle a matter of degree, reflecting the extent to which the associated roles are comprised of potentially conflicting norms and counter-norms. For example, in advanced societies, patients commonly expect their physicians to adopt both a dominant norm of emotional detachment and a subsidiary norm of compassion.[1] An equivalent principle applies to the compatibility of the rules across institutional domains (e.g., between the economy and the family). The degree to which the rules of the game within one domain directly contravene, override, or render obsolete those in other domains is a key indicator of the structural (mal)integration of social institutions, a potential source of social disorder, and a harbinger of social change.

A second dimension of social institutions – institutional regulation – refers to the basis of compliance with the rules of the game. Not all action in conformity with institutional norms is 'institutionalized' in the formal sense of the term. For example, actors might align their behaviour with the rules of the game based on utilitarian considerations of self-interest (Parsons, 1990 [1934]: 332–3) or in response to coercive pressures exerted by the more powerful. The distinctive feature of *institutionalized* social action is that it is governed by a sense of mutual obligation; actors align their behaviour with the rules of the game because they believe it is the right thing to do. Institutions therefore act as safeguards against purely opportunistic behaviour by encouraging attachments among individuals as well as commitment to the institution.

---

[1] This example is taken from Merton's (1976: 18) discussion of 'sociological ambivalence'.

In other words, when institutional regulation is strong, the rules of the game are awarded considerable *moral* authority or legitimacy.[2]

The third dimension of social institutions is that of institutional performance. As noted above, social institutions can be conceptualized with reference to the basic functions that they perform for society, that is, the socially beneficial outcomes to be realized as a result of the regulation of behaviour. Institutional performance refers to the extent to which commitment to and the faithful enactment of institutional roles result in the collectively desired institutional outcomes.

Although the three dimensions of institutions are analytically distinct, they are likely to be intimately interrelated. To illustrate these interconnections and the potential responses of institutions to changing circumstances, consider the institution of the economy in a hypothetical society. At one point in time, the rules governing economic activity coalesce into a governmentally directed command economy (the institutional *structure*). People align their economic behaviours closely with the economic rules of the game because they believe that such behaviours are proper and appropriate. The institutional *regulation* of the economy, in other words, is strong, and the economic rules of the game are awarded a high degree of moral authority. Institutional *performance* is also strong: the economy succeeds in producing goods and services at levels that are regarded as acceptable by prevailing standards.

Assume that a change in the environment – either natural or social – significantly impedes the capacity of the economy as organized to produce goods and services. Although people might initially continue to enact economic roles faithfully, institutional performance declines. It seems plausible to anticipate that, over time, poor institutional performance will tend to undermine the moral authority of the economic norms as the economy, in essence, fails 'to deliver the goods'. Institutional regulation will accordingly weaken, as will commitment. Furthermore, as the moral foundations of economic institutions are challenged, people are likely to entertain the possibility of alternative

---

[2] Some organizations, however, may seek to 'institutionalize' behaviours that contravene broader institutional values and norms and punish 'whistleblowers' who call attention to the resulting misbehaviour. See, for example, Jackall (1988) and Gobert and Punch (2000).

economic arrangements, perhaps those embodied in a market economy, and try to implement such arrangements. Depending on the success of such efforts, the end result could be the transformation of the institutional structure of the economy; qualitatively different rules of the game are instituted.

In sum, the institutional order of concrete societies can be usefully described with reference to these three, analytically distinct but empirically interrelated, dimensions: institutional structure, institutional regulation, and institutional performance. In the following section, we summarize a theoretical approach that applies these conceptual tools to explain variation in levels of crime across large-scale social systems: institutional-anomie theory.

Institutional-anomie theory

Institutional-anomie theory takes as its point of departure the fundamental insight about institutional structure discussed above, namely, that the degree of compatibility of the 'rules of the game' is in principle variable. This reflects a paradox that is inherent in any institutional order – the simultaneous interdependence and tension among institutions. Institutions are interdependent in the sense that the functioning of any one depends to some extent on the functioning of others. Recognition of such interdependence is implicit in Durkheim's insight regarding the role of 'non-contractual solidarities' in market transactions. Durkheim observes that economic activity always occurs within a context of pre-existing understandings and expectations, that is, within a larger non-economic institutional context. In a similar vein, Polanyi has used the concept of 'embeddedness' to characterize the interconnections between economic institutions and non-economic institutions:

> The human economy is embedded and enmeshed in institutions, economic and non-economic. The inclusion of the non-economic is vital. For religion or government may be as important to the structure and functioning of the economy as monetary institutions or the availability of tools and machines themselves that lighten the toil of labor (quoted in Smelser and Swedberg 1994: 15; see also Granovetter, 1985).

Despite the necessary interdependence of major social institutions, however, their integration is inherently problematic in any complex society.[3] There is always a certain degree of conflict or tension between them because the claims of some institutional roles will inevitably differ from and often contradict those of others. For example, the value orientations and associated demands of economic roles, especially in market-oriented societies, are not easily reconciled with those of familial roles. Traditionally for women and increasingly for men, being a 'good parent' at times must come at the expense of being a 'valued employee', and vice versa. The resolutions of these conflicting claims and obligations in the course of ongoing social interaction yield a distinctive pattern of institutional relationships for the society at large. We have referred to the outcome of this balancing of competing institutional claims as the 'institutional balance of power' in a society (Messner and Rosenfeld, 2007a: 74–84).

The type of institutional structure that is likely to generate high levels of crime in market capitalist societies is one in which the economy dominates the institutional balance of power.[4] Such economic dominance in the institutional balance of power is manifested in at least three important ways. First, non-economic functions and roles tend to be devalued in comparison with economic ones. Social success is defined and measured primarily in terms of market achievements. Second, non-economic roles typically must be accommodated to the requirements of economic roles when conflicts arise. The schedules, routines and demands of the workplace take precedence over those of the home, school, church, and community organization. Finally, economic standards and norms penetrate into non-economic realms. The market economy reproduces itself in other institutions to the extent that its calculating, utilitarian, efficiency-oriented logic informs

---

[3] In addition to the potentially problematic integration among social institutions, the structural arrangements that emerge to perform institutional functions might conflict with commonly shared value commitments in concrete societies. Law enforcement agencies, for example, might establish regularized patterns of behaviour (e.g., corruption, brutality) that run counter to collectively held values.

[4] See Rosenfeld and Messner (2006) for a speculative discussion of how forms of institutional imbalance other than economic dominance might be related to distinctive levels and types of crime.

conceptions of the means and ends of non-economic aspects of social life. Schwartz describes in some detail how 'our language is suffused with market terminology':

> The university is a 'free marketplace of ideas'. We 'spend' time with our friends. Athletes who want to succeed must be willing to 'pay the price' of rigorous training. We 'invest' a great deal in our children. We enter into marriage 'contracts'. (1994: 359–60)

In all of these ways, the market economy subjects other institutions to its own ends and converts the societies it dominates into 'market societies' (see Currie, 1991).

How does this type of institutional *structure* – one dominated by the economy – contribute specifically to crime? The answer provided by institutional-anomie theory involves two interrelated processes that involve the dimensions of institutions explained above. Economic dominance interferes with aspects of the *performance* of non-economic institutions that bear directly on criminal behaviour. Specifically, economic dominance erodes the structural restraints and social supports of non-economic institutions that would otherwise serve to inhibit crime. At the same time, economic dominance stimulates the growth of cultural pressures that ultimately undermine the moral *regulation* of institutions, resulting in a condition commonly referred to as 'anomie'.

Impaired institutional performance: the erosion of social control and social support

An important function of all social institutions is to align the behaviour of actors with the main cultural patterns of the society (Parsons, 1951). This is the essence of social control and a key benefit of social support, defined as the provision of the material and social resources needed to fulfill role obligations and achieve some measure of personal satisfaction (see Cullen and Wright, 1997). A strong institution is one that imposes effective controls over persons involved in its specific functional tasks and offers incentives for faithful conformity to role requirements. Economic dominance signals the evisceration of non-economic institutions. As non-economic institutions are devalued, forced to accommodate to economic imperatives, and ever more penetrated by market criteria, they are less able to perform their distinctive functions effectively, including those of social control and support. Feeble institutions do not offer attractive roles to which individuals are likely to become strongly attached or in which they will want to invest. As a consequence, the bonds to such conventional institutions will be tenuous, and the constraints against crime and the incentives for conformity associated with these bonds will be weak (Hirschi, 1969).

Economic dominance has important implications not only for the functioning of non-economic institutions but also for the nature of economic activity itself. An important theme of contemporary scholarship on markets is that economic activity occurs within a broader cultural and social context (Fourcade and Healy, 2007). Markets operate in, and to some degree are shaped by, non-market social relations. As Granovetter (1985: 490) observes, economic action is always 'overlaid' with social content and is embedded in networks of ongoing social interaction. When economic action is embedded in this sense, social control is strengthened, and economic action itself tends to curb egoistic impulses to pursue narrow self-interest. When the economy dominates other institutions, economic transactions occur to a greater extent without the tempering influence of the countervailing claims of other institutions. Ironically, then, an institutional balance of power characterized by economic dominance undermines the social control and support functions of all institutions – economic and non-economic alike.

Cultural pressures, an anomic ethic, and institutional regulation

Economic dominance also promotes high levels of crime by promoting cultural goals and values that weaken institutional regulation, that is, the moral authority of the rules of the game. To understand these pressures, it is useful to consider the distinctive value complex that characterizes market societies. This complex stresses individual competition as the primary basis for allocating social rewards. It also defines success in economic terms, thereby encouraging individuals to orient their behaviour toward the pursuit of monetary rewards. These market values and their accompanying behavioural guidelines socialize people in appropriate market behaviours and bestow legitimacy on markets as essential and desirable mechanisms for producing and distributing goods and services. Accordingly, a strong cultural emphasis on competition for monetary rewards is a functional requisite for the long-run viability of a market society.

There is nothing inherently criminogenic about the market values of competition and materialism. The pursuit of individual interests in competition with others can promote relationships of mutual obligation and trust, which are likely to inhibit 'malfeasance' (Granovetter, 1985). The market values of competition and materialism lead to crime, we suggest, only when they occur in combination with what can be termed an 'anomic ethic'. Following Merton (1968) the anomic ethic refers to the excessive emphasis on the goals of social action regardless of the moral status of the means used to achieve social goals. Under this cultural condition, persons are encouraged to use whatever means are technically most expedient to attain highly valued goals, notably but not exclusively the goal of economic success.

Anomie in this sense refers to more than the absence of social rules, as in the common definition of anomie as 'normlessness'. It is itself a social rule or standard, albeit a highly permissive one, that motivates the pursuit of goals 'by any means necessary'. As used in institutional-anomie theory, then, anomie does not result simply from the absence of culture but instead reflects a strong cultural emphasis on ends over means (cf. Orru, 1987).

Unlike the value placed on the competitive pursuit of monetary success through the market, the ethic of anomie has a very direct relationship with criminal behaviour and punitive social control. Persons who pursue goals by any means necessary have no *moral* qualms about using criminal means. The selection of means turns entirely on utilitarian, cost–benefit calculations, which include the perceived probability and severity of the penalties for criminal behaviour. Hence, persons in an anomic environment may prefer to use legal rather than illegal means to achieve a goal, but this preference is not rooted in the cultural prohibition of illegal means. In other words, the selection of the legal means has little expressive or ritual significance – is not viewed as good or right in itself – but results instead from an instrumental calculation that, in this particular situation, 'crime does not pay'.

Unlike the values of competition and materialism, which receive strong emphasis in all market societies, the anomic ethic is not a functional requisite of a market economy. Accordingly, the intensity and pervasiveness of anomie vary considerably across market contexts. Weber's (1976 [1904–05]) classic discussion of the functions of the Protestant Ethic in the early stages of capitalist development provides a good illustration of the analytic independence of anomie and market arrangements. Weber's early capitalists were strongly motivated to compete for monetary rewards, but they were also very sensitive to the legitimacy of the means by which the rewards are acquired and used. Indeed, the Protestant Ethic is often used interchangeably with the 'work ethic', a term that explicitly emphasizes the legitimate means and attendant personal qualities for acquiring and deploying wealth: dedication to task, deferred gratification, industriousness – in short, hard work. According to this ethic, wealth is the reward for hard work in a calling; it is not the only or even the primary reason for work. The economic rewards of work are to be reinvested in productive activity for the greater good of the community, as well as for the benefit – in this life and afterward – of the individual producer.

The Protestant Ethic accompanying early capitalism contrasts starkly with the anomic ethic as we have described it. The anomic ethic by definition is indifferent to the moral status of the means used to secure economic ends, and it encourages people to think only of themselves as they acquire money to secure and display personal worth and social status. But, as critics of capitalism allege, does the work ethic inevitably become emptied of broader cultural significance and degenerate into the ethic of anomie in the course of capitalist development?

We maintain that an important factor associated with the declining significance of the Protestant Ethic, and its replacement by the ethic of anomie, is the degree to which the economy dominates the institutional balance of power. The common function of non-economic institutions is to confer moral legitimacy on the means of social action. From a purely economic standpoint, technical efficiency is the sole criterion for evaluating the suitability of means. The presence of meaningful moral prohibitions against illegal behaviour, therefore, presupposes the existence of reasonably vital non-economic institutions. To the extent that the economy dominates other institutions, cultural messages that imbue the means of social action with moral significance lack institutional backing. Institutional *regulation* is weakened thereby. Under such conditions, the ethic of anomie will tend to emerge and promote high levels of criminality. It would seem that heavy reliance on punitive sanctions – police, courts and prisons – is the only way an anomic market society can keep criminal propensities in check.

Conclusion

We began this chapter by calling attention to a fundamental question that was at the core of much of the classical social thought that accompanied the development of capitalism as the predominant means for organizing economic activity. Does a capitalist market economy inevitably lead to social peace and harmony, or to moral collapse and disorder? Our answer is that the broader institutional context in which the market economy is embedded conditions the relationship between markets and morality. If non-economic institutions remain robust, they can prevent market values from degenerating into an anomic ethic which encourages the pursuit of self-interest by any means necessary. If non-economic institutions are devalued, inverted, and penetrated by the market economy, then the worst fears of critics of capitalism may well be realized.

We have applied these general propositions about anomic culture and institutional imbalance to the specific phenomenon of crime by means of institutional-anomie theory. The theory draws on other etiological perspectives but differs from nearly all of them in its focus on macro-level cultural patterns and social structures. As part of the 'new institutionalism' in criminology, institutional-anomie theory uses the tools of institutional analysis to explain the variation in crime rates across differing institutional orders. The overarching claim of the theory is that an institutional structure characterized by economic dominance impedes the social control and support functions of institutions which, when combined with an anomic cultural ethic, strips away the moral authority of these institutions and in so doing undermines institutional regulation. In other words, when the market economy dominates the institutional order, its rules and the values they reflect tend to prevail over those that would counterbalance market-oriented values and alleviate the impact of market conditions and outcomes on families and individuals. In the next chapter, we provide concrete illustrations of how the structure, regulation, and performance of economic institutions contribute to crime, as our focus turns from the lofty heights of theory to the nuts and bolts of empirical studies of the relationship between crime and the economy.

FOUR

understanding the economic context of crime in capitalist societies

In the middle of the last century, C. Wright Mills, a sociology professor at Columbia University, published a book that was destined to become a classic: *The Sociological Imagination*. Mills was a severe critic of the society of his time and of the dominant sociological approaches to the understanding of this society. With respect to the latter, he criticized two 'unfortunate tendencies' that he felt were dominant in the discipline of sociology and that stood in the way of realizing the promise of the sociological imagination (Mills, 1959: 22). He referred to these tendencies as 'grand theory' and 'abstracted empiricism'. In Mills's view, both entail a distorted connection between thinking and observing. Grand theory pursues the noble goal of constructing highly general explanations of social phenomena, but in so doing it operates at a level of thinking 'that is so general that its practitioners cannot logically get down to observation' (1959: 33). Abstracted empiricism, in contrast, makes a fetish of observation and the methods of observation, and as a result leaves little room for creative thinking. Mills (1959: 224) concluded his treatise with a plea for a sensible balance between abstract theorizing on the one hand and empirical observation on the other to foster fruitful intellectual craftsmanship.

In this chapter, we take Mills's advice to heart and put the abstract conceptualizing and theorizing that we introduced in the previous chapter to work to understand the social reality of crime in advanced capitalist societies. To reiterate the core ideas of our 'institutional perspective' very briefly, we have proposed that a society can be usefully described with reference to three basic features of social institutions – institutional structure, institutional regulation and institutional performance. Institutional structure refers to the content of social rules and their internal consistency. Institutional regulation refers to the moral authority that is awarded to institutional rules and thus the perceived legitimacy of institutional arrangements. Finally, institutional performance encompasses the 'outputs' of social institutions, that is, the extent to which the enactment of institutional roles results in collectively desired outcomes.

We have further proposed that these concepts can be applied to the specific phenomenon of crime in the form of institutional-anomie theory (IAT). The overarching claim of the theory is that the type of institutional structure in capitalist societies that tends to promote crime is one in which the economy dominates other social institutions. Such economic dominance influences criminal activity by means of two general social processes. On the one hand, economic dominance hinders the performance of non-economic institutions that have the responsibility for socializing people into the norms that are codified in criminal law. As a result, when persons select the means to secure any given end, the moral status of the means becomes increasingly irrelevant as a guide to action. Institutional regulation – adherence to the institutional rules on moral grounds – declines. The internalized restraints against crime are accordingly relatively weak, and individuals are 'free' to commit crimes. In this particular sense, economic dominance is associated with what might be termed a patterned deficiency in socialization. Economic dominance also has the ironic effect of generating a kind of hyper-socialization that has criminogenic consequences. Socialization into the habits and orientations that are expected of *market actors* is not deficient at all; on the contrary, it is exceedingly effective. As a result, the logic of the marketplace penetrates into non-economic domains, and people become highly attuned to calculative, cost–benefit considerations in the selection of means to achieve valued goals. This market mentality does not remain confined to purely economic transactions but tends to permeate social behaviour more generally. Unless it is checked by the moral norms of other institutions, a market mentality may degenerate into anomie and become a cultural source of crime.

These arguments advanced in IAT have implications for variation in both the levels and patterns of criminal activity in advanced capitalist societies that can be assessed with observations from the world around us. The theory implies that across societies with varying institutional structures, higher crime rates should be observed in those that have less effectively 'tamed the market'. Applying similar reasoning, societies that have experienced a rapid transition to a market economy and have not been able to establish strong non-economic institutions during this transition are likely to experience sharp increases in levels of crime. IAT also implies that the distinguishing features of crime will be closely related to the everyday working of the larger institutional order, that is, to institutional performance. Specifically, in a society characterized by economic dominance, criminal activity of all types is likely to bear striking resemblances to legitimate economic activity. Criminals, similar to other market actors, will orient their behaviour according to the cost–benefit schedules and opportunity structures in their social environment. In other words, across different forms of offences (street crimes, organized crimes, and white-collar crimes), the nature and rhythms of crime will mimic and be responsive to those of the larger institutional context. In the sections below, we demonstrate how levels, patterns, and the rhythms of crime can be understood more fully when viewed through the lens of an institutional perspective.

Crime and institutional structure: taming the market[1]

In the previous chapter, we extracted from the classical literature on social thought the fundamental insight that the consequences for the social and moral order of a society in which the economy is organized around capitalist markets are likely to be highly variable. Capitalist societies are not cut from the same cloth. They vary greatly with respect to the nature of social institutions and their interrelationships, reflecting prevailing cultural orientations and distinctive historical experiences.

---

[1] This section draws upon Messner and Rosenfeld (2000) and Messner et al. (2011).

The institutional economist Karl Polanyi (1957 [1944]) has called attention to one particularly important feature of the historical development of different capitalist societies: the extent to which they are able to establish viable political arrangements that provide public support for the welfare of their citizens.

Along with other prominent critics of capitalism, Polanyi emphasized the dangers of relying exclusively on markets for the organization of life, a situation that he referred to as the 'self-regulating market'. The self-regulating market, in his view, is a mythical, ideological construct that could never be realized because it would undermine the foundations for human existence. As he put it, 'robbed of the protective covering of cultural institutions, human beings would perish from the effects of social exposure' (Polanyi, 1957 [1944]: 73). Polanyi regarded the emergence of the modern welfare state as a critically important counterbalance to the otherwise self-destructive tendencies that tend to accompany the expansion of capitalist markets. The welfare state uses politically authorized redistributive mechanisms to enable citizens to meet their basic human needs for survival, independently of market considerations.

More recently, the sociologist Gøsta Esping-Andersen (1990) has extended Polanyi's arguments about the role of social welfare provisions as a counter-balance to the self-destructive tendencies of capitalist markets. Esping-Andersen observes that complete reliance on market arrangements for the satisfaction of the basic needs of everyday life implies that human labour power has become, in the Marxist expression, 'commodified'. In other words, it has become a commodity to be bought and sold on the market, similar to any other commercial good or service. Moreover, insofar as labour has become commodified, personal well-being depends on the market value of a person's labour power. Social welfare provisions given by the state provide alternative means for meeting basic needs and, in so doing, promote 'de-commodification'.

Esping-Anderson's notion of de-commodification can be readily translated into the terminology of IAT and applied to yield a testable hypothesis about variation in levels of crime across capitalist societies. De-commodification presupposes a balance between the state and the economy. The state is able to exercise its political authority to redistribute resources and promote the welfare of the population. It is, in other words, able to tame the market. In contrast, economic dominance by definition implies that other social institutions – including the state – are subservient to the market. From the vantage point of IAT, then, we should expect crime rates to be lower in societies where the social-welfare functions of the polity and the accompanying de-commodification policies are stronger – societies where the economy and the polity are more equally balanced – than in societies characterized by economic dominance.

We tested this expectation with data from a sample of industrial and post-industrial nations (Messner and Rosenfeld, 1997). We created a measure of de-commodification based on social welfare policies and estimated multivariate statistical models predicting homicide rates. Controlling for other influences on homicide, we found a significant relationship between national homicide rates and the de-commodification measure. Nations with more extensive and generous policies have lower homicide rates than those with more limited policies. This result held regardless of whether or not the United States – the clear leader in homicide – was included in the sample.

In subsequent cross-national research, Savolainen (2000) replicated the results of our study for a larger sample of nations and extended our analysis by considering whether social welfare policies condition the effect of income inequality on homicide. Cross-national research has consistently revealed a robust, positive relationship between homicide and income inequality (Messner et al., 2002, 2010). Drawing from IAT, Savolainen (2000) reasoned that the impact of income inequality on homicide should be weaker in nations where the institution of the economy is less dominant over the polity and, accordingly, their citizens are afforded greater protection from market forces. This expectation was supported in the analysis. Applying similar reasoning, in a later study we found that the relationship between unemployment and homicide rates is weaker in nations with more extensive social welfare policies than in those with narrower and less generous policies (Rosenfeld and Messner, 2007).

These research findings, along with those of prior studies on homicide and the welfare state (e.g., Gartner, 1991; Pampel and Gartner, 1995; Savage et al., 2008), lend support to the prediction of IAT that strong welfare states – an indicator of greater balance between the institutions of the economy and polity – limit criminal homicide in advanced, industrial nations, both directly and indirectly by reducing the impact of other homicide determinants such as inequality and unemployment (see also Wilkinson and Pickett, 2009). Whether the same effects exist for crimes other than homicide remains an open and important empirical question for future cross-national research.

More broadly, the research to date underscores the significance of the *structure* of social institutions for explaining the variation in crime rates across differing institutional orders. The relative balance of the economy and political system is not a matter of institutional regulation or performance but of the rules that shape social action under differing institutional circumstances. When the free-market economy dominates the institutional order, its rules and the values they reflect tend to prevail over those that would counterbalance market-oriented values and alleviate the impact of market conditions and outcomes on families and individuals. These theoretical considerations, and the accompanying research, apply to the institutional structures of contemporary advanced capitalist societies. We now broaden the comparative lens and consider the criminogenic effects of the rapid transition to a market economy and democratic political order in post-Soviet Russia.

Crime and institutional regulation: 'wild capitalism' and anomie in post-soviet Russia

Not long after the Soviet Union fell in 1991, the Western press began reporting a sharp increase in crime in the 'new Russia'. The reports chronicled gruesome murders, frequent kidnappings, extortion schemes, protection rackets, blatant sexual harassment and violence, the influence of organized crime on newly privatized businesses, rampant government and police corruption, and a general rise in fear and anxiety in the population. Illustrative accounts include:

■ 'One day last month, St. Petersburg police found seven corpses: six of the victims had been stabbed in drug-related killings, and the seventh was tortured, burned, tied up with wire and left in a cemetery, the mob's favorite dumping ground' (Elliott, 1992: 50).

- 'Break-ins have caused a run on steel doors, iron gates and alarm systems. Security companies are thriving, although some are really racketeers whose offer to protect premises are accompanied by vague threats of the consequences if their services are refused' (Bohlen, 1992: 6).

- 'One of the few Russians to take up the battle against sexual harassment is a man. Valery V. Vikulov, 31, says he set up an underground organization ... to assist women who have lost their jobs as a result of sexual harassment. ... While most of the cases he has handled involve the loss of promotions, bonuses or jobs by women, a few are more extreme. Mr. Vikulov said he had helped one 19 year-old woman ... who said she was gang-raped by her employers after a dinner they held to celebrate her promotion' (Stanley, 1994: 7).

- '... a Moscow banker named Nikolai Likhachev leaves his home en route to work, but before he can reach the security detail waiting by his car, a man with a high-powered rifle shoots him dead. Likhachev had refused to pay more extortion money to a Russian mafia group' (Duffy and Trimble, 1994: 11–12).

What caused this precipitous rise in violence and mayhem in Russia after the fall of the Soviet system? The news accounts targeted a single culprit: capitalism, or as the press variously termed the new economic order, 'wild capitalism', 'cowboy capitalism', 'rough, raw capitalism', 'anything-goes capitalism', 'deadly capitalism'. The basic motif of the popular accounts of the new Russia was that the rush to privatization and free markets after the collapse of the old totalitarian system brought with it a pervasive distrust, a breakdown of collective sentiments, rampant individualism, a sense that the old rules no longer mattered and new ones either had not developed or could be broken with impunity – in a word, anomie. As one reporter put it:

> It is not just a matter of crime, corruption, prostitution, smuggling, and drug and alcohol abuse, although there is plenty of evidence that these are on the rise. There is also a widespread view that now, as Russia goes through another historic convulsion, people are out for themselves and anything goes. (Bohlen, 1992: 1)

At first glance, the moral entropy and criminal violence of post-Soviet Russia might seem to suggest that market arrangements naturally produce rampant egoism, moral decay, and social disorder. But that would be a one-sided view of a more complex social reality. The rush to capitalism did coincide with an abrupt rise in crime and breakdown in social control in Russia, but this is not a historical inevitability, nor was it the first time in Russian history that rapid institutional change had resulted in disorder and crime (Figes, 1996). Moreover, the reintegration of the former East Germany (the German Democratic Republic) into the modern German state entailed a rapid transformation from a state-run to a capitalist market economy with only modest, and rather short-lived, increases in crime in the territories of the former communist regime (Messner et al., 2012). In Russia, the speed of the transition combined with the absence of counterbalancing institutional forces, and not capitalism itself, led to widespread crime and a general sense of uncertainty and unease.

This interpretation is buttressed by a series of studies conducted by criminologist William Pridemore and colleagues. Media portrayals of crime often exaggerate crime increases, but Pridemore's research supports the press accounts of a precipitous rise in crime and violence after the fall of the Soviet Union. For example, Pridemore et al. (2007: 280) observed: 'There is little doubt that Russian homicide and suicide rates are noticeably higher after the breakup of the Soviet Union than before its demise.' They also documented comparable increases in alcohol-related death rates. The researchers attributed the rapid rise in violence and related problems to anomie. Specifically, they invoked Durkheim's (1964 [1893]) concept of the 'anomic division of labor' to explain how abrupt social change unleashes individual expectations and desires from values and norms that had held them in check. Summarizing Durkheim's argument, Pridemore et al. (2007: 274) maintained: 'This state of normlessness continues to foster crime and deviance until the cultural system adapts to the new social order, thereby re-establishing social equilibrium.'

Under the Soviet regime, Russians could count on a broad array of social services and protections – old age and military pensions, paid maternity leave, universal health care, free education, price controls on essential goods and services – which guaranteed a basic standard of living and lent support to group-oriented 'communitarian' values of Russian society that predated the Soviet era. Almost immediately after the fall of the Soviet state, the social safety net unravelled, leaving citizens 'unsheltered in the face of the transition and the new market economy' (Pridemore et al., 2007: 275–6). In addition, citizens were exposed to Western values stressing individualism, competition, and monetary accumulation which had been scorned just a few years before, resulting in cultural disorientation and uncertainty about the future. Finally, the 'new capitalistic emphasis on self-reliance and cash accumulation' threatened family and friendship networks (ibid: 276).[2]

The authors summarized their thesis in terms consonant with IAT: 'Traditional societal institutions were quickly subordinated to the economy, and many Russians began to feel alienated by their quest for personal financial security, since the search for it includes independence from, and even competition with, those on whom they once depended' (Pridemore et al., 2007: 276). Their empirical analysis of trends in homicide, suicide, and alcohol-related deaths supports their hypothesis that the breakup of the Soviet Union and consequent demise of traditional values, social structures, and political controls promoted increases in crime and disorder in post-Soviet Russia.

To repeat, capitalism itself is not the culprit in this story of rapid social change, anomie, and escalating crime and disorder in the new Russia. Rather, the abrupt *institutional deregulation* of Russian society and accompanying legitimization crisis rendered the old rules of the game irrelevant to new social circumstances. Along with the rise of a market economy, rapid democratization in the form of competitive elections and an emphasis on individual rights may have spurred increases in crime and violence. Pridemore and Kim (2006) examined this hypothesis in a study of regional homicide rates in Russia after the fall of the Soviet Union. Drawing on Durkheim's thesis that rapid political change increases homicide rates by threatening collective sentiments (1964 [1893]), they surmized that homicide rates should have

---

[2] The strength of families, the church, voluntary associations, and other civil institutions in the Soviet Union must not be exaggerated. The pogroms and mass slaughters under Stalin, and the widespread detentions and secret police throughout the period of Communist rule, are reminders that Russian civil society was threatened and deeply penetrated by the state.

risen more rapidly in regions that exhibited strong support for democratic political change than in those where support for a return to Soviet-style governance and society was greater. Controlling for regional differences in urbanization, socioeconomic disadvantage, educational attainment, and alcohol consumption, Pridemore and Kim found, consistent with their hypothesis, greater homicide increases in Russian regions where the electorate was more supportive of the political parties calling for democratic change.

Pridemore and Kim (2006) acknowledged several limitations of their study, notably the absence of a direct measure of collective sentiments and the difficulty in separating out the effects on homicide of democratization and 'marketization', both of which threatened traditional values and institutions. They also emphasized that democracy itself does not necessarily produce crime and disorder, at least over the long term. It was the rapidity of the political transition in Russia that, like the abrupt economic reforms, rendered traditional ways of life obsolete and the collective sentiments that gave them meaning suspect. The Russian case illustrates the sheer power of institutional deregulation, whereby the moral bases of behaviour atrophy and people struggle to attain goals by any means necessary. The moral of the story is that rapid social change without countervailing institutional controls – which in the nature of the case take time to develop – promotes institutional deregulation, anomie, and rising levels of crime.

Crime and institutional performance: the rhythms of the economy and the demand for crime

We have suggested that variations in the level of crime across societies can be linked to differences in societal institutional structures and that abrupt changes in crime within a society, such as those observed in post-Soviet Russia, often result from the demoralization that accompanies a decline in institutional regulation. We now turn to the connection between crime and institutional performance. In this section, we focus primarily on the case of the contemporary United States because the institutional order of US society is characterized by a particularly high degree of economic dominance, and thus the rhythms of the economy and crime are very closely attuned to one another. Recall that institutional performance refers to whether faithful enactment of institutional roles results in expected rewards. When persons perceive that playing by the existing rules of the game is rewarding, their motivation to engage in criminal behaviour should be weak. But when playing by the rules does not deliver the rewards to which persons believe they are entitled, criminal motivations are strengthened. It follows that variations in crime across places and over time should be connected to comparable variations in institutional performance.

Market economies are inherently dynamic. Their performance is tied to the inescapable ups and downs of economic output, profits, wages, prices, and employment. During periods of economic expansion, unemployment rates typically fall and real incomes rise. In other words, the rewards attached to legitimate economic roles increase, at least on average. But the history of market economies is a tale of economic booms followed by busts, which together constitute the 'rhythms' of market economies. During economic downturns, when unemployment rises and real incomes fall, legitimate economic pursuits become less rewarding, and some persons will turn to illegitimate means to pursue their economic goals.

We apply these and related ideas to three forms of criminal behaviour: street crime, organized crime, and white-collar crime. Street crimes include the murders, assaults, robberies, burglaries, and thefts that dominate the attention of law enforcement, the courts, policy-makers, the general public, and, for that matter, criminologists. The term 'organized crime' eludes precise definition, but generally refers to the supply of illegitimate goods and services by groups characterized by a relatively extensive division of labour and centralized command structure. The term 'white-collar crime' encompasses offences such as price fixing, fraud, embezzlement, and restraint of trade carried out by persons in conjunction with their legitimate occupational or organizational roles. The common characteristic emphasized in the discussion that follows is that all three forms of criminal offending are related to the *demand for crime* that varies, in turn, with the rhythms and regulatory environment of the market economy.

Street crime, inflation and the great recession

Inflation is the cruellest tax.

Unknown[3]

Until recently, the research literature on the relationship between economic performance and crime trends was puzzling at best and grim at worst. Puzzling because studies consistently returned mixed results. Grim because the results could be used to support almost any conclusion about how, or whether, the economy affects crime rates (Bushway, 2011; Rosenfeld, 2011a). Around the turn of the current century, however, the 'consensus of doubt' (Chiricos, 1987) began to give way to a new research consensus regarding the relationship between the economy and street crime.

The new consensus was fuelled, in part, by replacement or supplementation of the official unemployment rate, the longstanding economic indicator of choice in research on crime trends, with other economic indicators. Several studies confirmed the age-old belief that worsening economic conditions produce disorder and crime. A good bit of the groundwork for the recent research on the economy and crime was established in an early paper by Cook and Zarkin (1985), who found that rates of property crime, but not violent crime, tend to increase during recessions and decline during recoveries (see also Field, 1990). More recently, Arvanites and Defina (2006) found that state-level gross domestic product (GDP) per capita is significantly related to property crime trends in US states in the expected direction: As output falls, crime rates increase. They found no significant effect of unemployment on property crime, and no effect of either GDP or unemployment on violent crime. Rosenfeld and Fornango (2007) replicated these results and also found that collective perceptions of economic change, or 'consumer sentiment', are significantly associated with regional property crime trends (see also Lauritsen and Heimer, 2010). During periods of rising consumer confidence and optimism, crime rates fall, and when confidence wanes, crime rates rise. Similar

---

[3] This quotation has been attributed, variously, to Milton Friedman, Jimmy Carter, and Paul Volker, former chair of the Board of Governors of the Federal Reserve System, all without much confirmation.

results for the effects of consumer sentiment were reported in a comparative study of burglary rates in the US and nine European nations (Rosenfeld and Messner, 2009). Grogger (1998) and Gould et al. (2002) found an inverse relationship between wages and youth crime in the US. Finally, some studies showed the expected positive effect of unemployment on crime trends (e.g., Gould et al., 2002; Raphael and Winter-Ebmer, 2001).

And then came the 'Great Recession' of 2008 and 2009. Economic output plunged, unemployment soared, and consumer confidence hit a historical low point. But crime rates did not rise in response as they had in the past. In fact, the FBI's Uniform Crime Reports (UCR) reveal national decreases in both property and violent crime rates in 2008 and 2009, and the changes in UCR crime rates are mirrored by similar decreases in personal and household victimization measured by the National Crime Victimization Survey (NCVS), which are unaffected by variations in the rate at which crimes are reported to the police and police recording practices.[4]

It remains to be seen whether the absence of crime increases during the 2008–09 recession will reinstate the 'consensus of doubt' concerning the effect of economic conditions on crime. At the very least, the Great Recession poses a challenge to the new research consensus on crime and the economy. If deteriorating economic performance drives up crime, how are we to explain falling crime rates during a severe recession?

There is no disputing the gravity of the 2008–09 recession. By some measures, it was worse than all previous downturns since the Great Depression of the 1930s. Comparisons of the 2008–09 recession with the Great Depression are often overdrawn (see Temin, 2010). On one key economic indicator, however, the two crises are similar: consumer prices stagnated and fell in both periods. Price deflation was far greater during the first years of the Depression, but in 2009 consumer prices fell for the first time in over 50 years. Although price increases often slow during recessions, they rarely turn negative. That has happened only

---

[4] UCR property and violent crime rates dropped by 7% and 9%, respectively, over the two years (http://www2.fbi.gov/ucr/cius2009/data/table_01.html). NCVS crime data are available at http://bjs.ojp.usdoj.gov/index.cfm?ty=pbdetail&iid=2218.

three times in the 12 officially-recorded recessions in the US since the Great Depression: in 1949, 1954 and 2009.[5]

If the 2008–09 recession differs from most others in price behaviour, what relevance does this have for criminal behaviour? A suggestive historical case can be made that changing crime rates coincide with price changes. As prices fell during the 1930s, crime rates did as well. We might then add price deflation to the list of proposed solutions to the riddle of why crime dropped during the Great Depression (see, for example, Johnson et al., 2007). Both crime and consumer prices were at historic lows during the 1950s. And what of the paradox of 'crime amidst plenty' in the 1960s (Wilson, 1985)? In fact, prices began a steep rise in the mid-1960s, and crime rates followed suit (see LaFree, 1998). While intriguing, these historical parallels offer only impressionistic evidence of the connection between inflation and crime. The connection is supported, however, by more systematic empirical studies, although the relevant research is modest in both size and theoretical depth.

Several studies report a significant and positive association between inflation and crime rates in the US. Tang and Lean (2007) found a positive relationship between inflation and crime rates for the period 1960 to 2005 and concluded that the causal direction of the association is from inflation to crime. Allen (1996) examined the effects of inflation and several other socio-economic indicators in time-series models of robbery, burglary, and motor vehicle theft rates between 1959 and 1992. The study reports a significant and positive inflation effect on all three offence types and concludes that 'inflation motivates criminal behaviour independently of other socio-economic conditions' (1996: 303). Ralston (1999) reported a similar result for inflation in an analysis of burglary, larceny, and motor vehicle theft rates between 1958 and 1995 (see also Cohen and Felson, 1979).

We illustrate the relationship between inflation and 'acquisitive' crime in Figure 4.1. The measure of acquisitive crime includes the UCR offences of robbery, burglary, larceny, and motor vehicle theft; all are crimes committed to obtain money or property from the victim. The

---

[5] The price data are from the Bureau of Labor Statistics (ftp://ftp.bls.gov/pub/special. requests/cpi/cpiai.txt). The dates of US recessions are from the National Bureau of Economic Research (http://www.nber.org/cycles/cyclesmain.html).

inflation measure is based on the All Items Consumer Price Index for All Urban Consumers (CPI-U) from the Bureau of Labor Statistics (http://www.bls.gov/bls/inflation.htm). The CPI-U is the broadest and most comprehensive consumer price information available, consisting of over 200 categories of goods and services and covering about 87% of the US population.

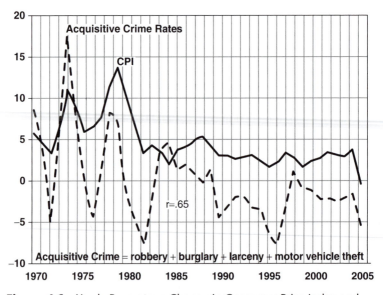

Figure 4.1 Yearly Percentage Change in Consumer Price Index and Acquisitive Crimes per 100,000 Population, 1970–2009.

The figure depicts a moderately strong positive relationship between the yearly percentage change in inflation and acquisitive crime in the United States between 1970 and 2009 (r = .65). The relationship is particularly pronounced during the early years of the period when inflation rates were running at very high levels. Inflation has moderated in the United States since then, as have crime rates. Both inflation and acquisitive crime dropped sharply in 2009, well into the Great Recession.

In most studies of inflation and crime, inflation is included as a control variable or as one of several measures of economic distress, without much theoretical development. An exception is an early study by Devine et al. (1988) that considers inflation and unemployment to be the two main macro-economic indicators that influence US crime trends. The researchers argued that 'inflation unleashes distributional conflict and undermines confidence in existing institutional arrangements' (p. 408). This point is echoed in LaFree's (1998) account of the role of inflation in increasing crime by eroding institutional legitimacy. These arguments highlight the effects of inflation in undermining institutional regulation, but they do not exhaust the theoretical significance of inflation as a cause of crime. Inflation is also a sign of diminished institutional performance. Fluctuation in the price of goods and services is a normal property of market economies. Price changes affect crime rates, we argue, by influencing consumer demand for cheap stolen goods.

The dynamics of demand and control in underground markets

Persons engaged in income-producing crime must have a way of disposing of the goods they steal that they do not consume. They can give them away, sell them for cash, or exchange them for something else of value. Gifts aside, property offenders perforce must become involved in underground or 'off-the-books' transactions because it is illegal to buy and sell stolen goods. Applying standard economic theory, the greater the demand for stolen goods, the higher are the returns to acquisitive crime (Ehrlich, 1973). The key issue in understanding the influence of illegal markets on crime, then, concerns the conditions that shape the demand for stolen goods.

Research on illicit drug markets has considered their demand characteristics in some detail (Reuter, 2010). Research on markets for stolen goods is more limited, especially with respect to how changes in the formal economy affect their expansion and contraction over time. Obtaining systematic time-series data on such markets is difficult, of course, because detailed records are rarely kept, but relevant insights can be drawn from observations of change in the retail sector of the formal economy. Generally speaking, when aggregate incomes fall or prices rise, consumers search for cheaper goods and services, a phenomenon economists refer to as 'trading down'. For example, as prices increase, mid-level retail outlets typically lose customers to those selling the same or similar goods at discount prices, such as Walmart and other 'big-box' discount outlets, 'dollar' stores, and the retail shops operated by Goodwill Industries and the Salvation Army. As a result, such businesses do comparatively well during economic downturns (Associated Press, 2011; Burke, 2008; Jackson and Feld, 2011; Rosenbloom, 2008).

But where do those who had been shopping at Dollar General or Goodwill trade down when the economy sours? Although the evidence trail leaves off at the bottom rungs of the formal retail market, a reasonable inference from the foregoing is that some enter the underground economy, including the market for stolen goods, in search of lower prices. The cardinal quality of stolen merchandise is that it is cheap. If it were not, it would attract few consumers away from legal markets that sell the same products with purity and quality guarantees, return and replacement policies, peaceful procedures for resolving disputes, and no risk of arrest.

Stolen goods are not only cheap in comparison to the same or equivalent merchandise purchased legally, they are 'inferior goods'. In economic theory, inferior goods differ from normal goods not necessarily on the basis of quality but with respect to their demand characteristics. Unlike normal goods, the demand for inferior goods rises as aggregate real income falls (see, for example, Mankiw, 2009: 466–7, 851). The second-hand clothing, furniture, toys, and electronic goods marketed at yard sales, pawnshops, and rent-to-own outlets are inferior goods. So are used cars, inexpensive foodstuffs, irregular and 'knock-off' clothing, and many varieties of costume jewellery. Stolen goods may be new or used, of superior or wretched quality, but demand for stolen goods, like all inferior goods, is greatest among those of modest means (Sutton, 1995, 1998). When prices rise or incomes fall, the population of such consumers grows.

A staple of economic theories of crime is that offenders respond to incentives (Becker, 1968; Ehrlich, 1973). Rising demand for inferior goods, therefore, should strengthen incentives for those who supply underground markets with such merchandise acquired through robbery, burglary, and theft. Property crime rates should increase as a result. Moreover, as illegal markets expand and transactions in stolen merchandise multiply, we should also expect to observe increases in violent crime.

Illegal commerce can be risky business. It is apt to occur after hours and in out-of-the-way places beyond the scrutiny of the police and other agents of formal social control (Venkatesh, 2006). When disputes arise between buyers and sellers of stolen goods, they cannot be handled by store managers, customer service departments, credit agencies, consumer advocates, or the courts. In such 'stateless' social contexts, violence is used to enforce agreements and punish wrongdoers. In addition, the legal vulnerability of the participants in illegal transactions makes them attractive targets of predatory crime (e.g., Jacobs, 2000).[6] These observations are now commonplace in the study of violence associated with illicit drug markets, but they apply in principle to any market arrangement in which participants have little access to formal social control and are vulnerable to predation.

The demand for inferior goods increases, as noted, when prices rise or incomes fall. Recent research documenting a connection between deteriorating economic performance and crime increases has focused on conditions that result in declines in income, such as unemployment and weak economic growth, and devoted little attention to price increases. The small and scattered literature on crime and inflation has not been incorporated in the new research consensus on the economy and crime. But if the economic logic linking the market for stolen goods to property and violent crime is sound, inflation should matter as much or more in the study of crime trends as unemployment, GDP, or income.

In contrast with unemployment, the effects of inflation are widespread, instantaneous, and direct. The official unemployment rate, which excludes discouraged workers and others who have dropped out of the labour force, is a narrow and incomplete measure of joblessness (http://www.bls.gov/cps/cps_htgm.htm#unemployed). But even broader measures such as labour-force participation necessarily apply only to persons who are out of work (and their families) and do not capture the effects of changing economic conditions on those who remain employed, who constitute the large majority of the working-age population even

---

[6] In a longitudinal study of Pittsburgh youth, Loeber and Farrington (2011) found that possession of stolen goods is a robust predictor of subsequent homicide victimization.

under the worst economic circumstances. In addition, the full effects of job loss typically develop over a period of months, as savings are drawn down and unemployment insurance benefits are exhausted (Cantor and Land, 1985). By contrast, although its effects are greatest for the poor (Easterly and Fischer, 2001), inflation touches all consumers. And its impact is felt immediately: yesterday's price increases affect today's purchases.

Compared with those of inflation, the effects of unemployment, GDP, and even income on the demand for stolen goods are less direct and more conditional. Unemployment influences consumer demand primarily to the extent that it reduces income. The effect of overall economic output and growth on demand is even less direct. Income obviously has a very close connection to demand, but only insofar as it keeps pace with prices. If price increases exceed income growth and real income declines, demand for normal goods should fall, demand for inferior goods should rise, and, according to the logic model advanced here, crime rates should increase.

We have focused on a single mechanism – underground markets – to interpret the contribution of inflation to year-to-year changes in crime rates. That is both a strength and limitation of our discussion of how crime is affected by the performance of the economy. The strength entails theoretical elaboration of how price changes influence crime by altering the dynamics of underground markets. The limitation is the lack of direct empirical indicators of price changes in such markets.

With an absence of this information, the next-best option is to derive inferences regarding demand in illegal markets from consumer behaviour at the lowest rungs of the formal retail market and from research on illicit drug markets – the approach we have taken. Conclusions must remain provisional, however, until more direct evidence on the temporal dynamics of demand and control in illegal markets becomes available. Meanwhile, it seems reasonable to conclude that adding inflation to the repertoire of macro-economic indicators used in the study of crime can yield new insights and help to resolve empirical anomalies, such as why crime rates drop when other indicators suggest they should increase. It is not yet time for theory and research on the economy and street crime to succumb to a new consensus of doubt.

Organized and white-collar crime: the over- and under-regulation of demand

Not all crime, of course, is a response to market demand. There is no 'demand' for the anger, hate, and jealousy that can lead to homicide. Yet, as we have argued, the dynamics of consumer demand play an important role in the production of crime by market economies. Put simply, 'demand' refers to the willingness of consumers to purchase a commodity at a given price. Governments seek to regulate consumer demand through fiscal and monetary policy, educational and public-health programmes, and the legal control of business activity. In some cases, governments try to stimulate demand, for example, by declaring 'tax holidays' or providing tax breaks on loans to purchase a home. In other instances, officials try to suppress demand by, for example, issuing warnings about the risks of consuming too much fat, alcohol, or tobacco. At the extreme, policies are instituted that outlaw the possession of particular commodities. Nearly every developed nation, for example, currently prohibits or severely restricts the possession, sale, and manufacture of particular psychoactive drugs, including heroin, cocaine and, in most cases, marijuana. At the other extreme, governments permit unlimited access to commodities or subject them to minimal health and safety regulations. In such cases, consumer preferences and price are the main determinants of demand.

We have suggested that the retail price of commodities that consumers desire influences the market for stolen goods. When commodity prices rise or real incomes fall, consumers trade down in search of substitutes available at lower prices, and some enter the market for stolen goods, which increases the rate of property crime. These considerations apply to legal commodities. It is not unlawful to possess jewellery, furniture, or electronic goods; the law proscribes only the particular means by which they are acquired, notably theft and receipt of stolen property.

But other commodities are illegal to possess no matter how they are acquired. Such *illicit commodities* are creatures of government policies. The ultimate aim of these policies is to reduce the consumption of commodities considered especially harmful, such as the psychoactive drugs mentioned earlier. But if demand remains strong, prohibitionist policies may have the unintended consequence of generating an underground market in illicit commodities and incentives for criminal groups to supply them. Illicit commodities, then, are products of what Merton (1936) called the 'unintended consequences of purposive social action'. Organized crime is in large measure a response to the demand for illicit commodities borne of government policy.

We will term policies that generate underground markets in illicit commodities policies of *over-regulation*. Over-regulation policies can create prime breeding grounds for organized crime. On the other hand, the *under-regulation* of market activity can also produce crime, including the white-collar crimes committed by persons in performance of their occupational or organizational roles. Very often such policies are not designed to affect demand directly. Rather, they aim to reduce or extinguish the supply of particular commodities, in the case of over-regulation, or to eliminate impediments to supply, in the case of under-regulation. But the ultimate purpose of nearly all 'supply-side' policies is to raise or lower the effective price of commodities to consumers on the assumption that higher prices will reduce consumer demand and lower prices will increase it. To illustrate the criminogenic consequences of over-regulation, we discuss the connection between organized crime and the market for illicit drugs. We then discuss the housing and financial crises of 2008 and 2009, and the white-collar crimes that contributed to them, as the unintended consequences of under-regulation.

Illicit drugs and organized crime

All I do is supply a public demand.
Al Capone[7]

When the Eighteenth Amendment to the Constitution was ratified in 1919, alcohol became an illicit commodity in the United States. The amendment, which outlawed the manufacture, transportation, and sale of 'intoxicating liquours', was repealed just 14 years later in 1933, despite the fact that alcohol consumption had dropped since ratification (Miron and Zwiebel, 1991). Although many interests lined up

---

[7] Quoted in Kenney and Finckenauer (1995: 155).

behind repeal, a major impetus was the perceived threat of the criminal enterprises that had taken over the liquor trade during 'Prohibition'.

Organized crime predated the Eighteenth Amendment, but Prohibition offered unparalleled opportunities for expansion and profit, secured when necessary by corruption and violence. Throughout the 1920s, newspapers, newsreels, and radio reported on politicians on the payroll of racketeers, police raids on 'speakeasies' selling illegal alcohol, and gang wars by groups vying for local and regional control of the underground commerce in liquour and beer. The most famous episode of gang violence during Prohibition is the 'St. Valentine's Day Massacre' of 1929 in which seven members of a North Side Chicago gang were murdered, execution style, by South Side rivals, some dressed as police officers, at the headquarters of a local beer distributor. The press wasted no time in framing the event as the violent outgrowth of Prohibition: 'The killings have stunned the citizenry of Chicago as well as the Police Department, and while tonight there was no solution, the one outstanding cause was illicit liquor traffic' (*New York Times*, 1929). The rise in violence during Prohibition, however, was not simply a media creation. Homicide rates increased during the 1920s and then fell immediately after repeal in 1933. Studies of early twentieth-century homicide trends have linked them to Prohibition (Miron, 1999; Owens, 2011).

Prohibition reveals a telling irony of over-regulation: when desired commodities and the industries that supply them are outlawed and driven into the underground economy, formal regulation of business activity ceases. Without recourse to legitimate means for resolving disputes over ownership, price and profits, underground entrepreneurs use violence to enforce contracts, gain territory, acquire product, set prices, fend off competitors, and protect against predators. The only means the state has at its disposal for controlling the violence is enforcement of the criminal law. But if demand for illicit commodities remains strong, the rigorous enforcement of prohibitionist policies may simply drive illicit commerce further underground and attract even more irresponsible entrepreneurs and violent predators into the market. This seems to have happened a half century after Prohibition ended when the United States declared a 'war on drugs'.

The United States experienced a sharp upswing in homicide during the 1980s.[8] Nearly all of the increase was driven by an explosive growth in rates of youth homicide, particularly among African-American males, first in the larger cities and then spreading to smaller ones. Moreover, the upturn in homicide was confined to killings with guns (Blumstein, 2006; Blumstein and Rosenfeld, 1998; Cook and Laub, 1998).

After peaking in the early 1990s, homicide rates began to fall and by 2000 were more than 40% below their 1991 peak levels. The drop in serious criminal violence mirrored the increase: it occurred first in the largest cities and spread later to the smaller ones; it was most pronounced among young African-American males; and it was concentrated in the firearm category (Blumstein and Rosenfeld, 2008; Cook and Laub, 2002).

Blumstein (1995, 2006) highlighted these age and race differences in homicide trends to support his argument that the youth homicide rise resulted from the expansion of the urban crack markets beginning in the mid-1980s, as young sellers were recruited into the markets to replace older drug dealers, who faced a heightened risk of incarceration during the nation's war on drugs. They acquired firearms for protection against rival sellers and street robbers, driving up the incentive for other inner-city youth, not necessarily connected to the drug markets, to arm themselves in an increasingly threatening environment. That environment also became a prime recruiting ground for urban street gangs. A classic arms race began, and firearm violence diffused away from the drug markets. As the crack epidemic began to abate in the early 1990s, levels of firearm violence fell as well, with some lag due to the self-perpetuating, 'contagious' quality of an arms race.

Studies by other researchers lend support to Blumstein's hypothesis linking late twentieth-century trends in youth homicide in the United States to the dynamics of urban drug markets. Sheley and Wright (1995) reported survey evidence connecting drug-market activity with firearm possession by inner-city adolescents. Cork (1999) found that the rise and fall of drug-market activity in US cities preceded the corresponding increase and decline of youth firearm violence. Using urinalysis data to

---

[8] Parts of this section are adapted from Messner and Rosenfeld (2007a) and Rosenfeld (2011a).

document the drug use of persons arrested for misdemeanours and felonies in US cities, Golub and Johnson (1997) showed that the upsurge, peak and decline in cocaine use by criminal suspects tended to occur first in the larger coastal cities and one or more years later in the smaller cities (see also Messner et al., 2005; Ousey and Lee, 2002).

A great deal of suggestive evidence, therefore, points to inner-city crack markets as the staging ground for the rise during the 1980s of serious youth violence in the United States. What attracted many inner-city young men to an enterprise that they clearly knew carried great legal and physical risk? An ethnographic study of crack sellers concludes that selling drugs has three major attractions for inner-city youth: the promise of easy money, autonomy from the dull and confining routines of available legitimate work, and for some, addiction to the drug itself (Jacobs, 1999: 26–42). In the US, for young men with few skills and limited prospects, selling drugs is a way of securing the 'American dream', and it bears undeniable similarities to other, more legitimate paths to success. 'Except for the fact that it is illegal,' noted one ethnographer, 'selling drugs is much like selling anything else' (Sullivan, 1989: 239). William Adler's account of the Chambers brothers, who ran a highly lucrative crack business in Detroit during the 1980s, compares their pursuit of financial gain with that of 'mainstream capitalists': 'Like any successful entrepreneurs, they identified a niche in the marketplace, assessed the barriers to entry, learned how to buy wholesale, mass-produce and market their product and track inventory.' If the tools of their trade differed from those of legitimate businesses – they 'broke knees and heads, shot people, burned houses' – their goals did not (Adler, 1995: 6–7; for a similar account, see Bourgois, 1995).

As the crack epidemic crested and declined, the illegitimate opportunities for 'making it' through drug-selling also diminished. Fortunately, opportunities within the legitimate economy began to grow at the same time, as the United States entered a period of record economic expansion in the 1990s. The role of opportunities in the legitimate labour market interacts in complex ways with changes in the illicit opportunity structure of distressed urban communities. The availability of low-wage jobs in the secondary labour market is particularly relevant when illicit markets and the employment opportunities they offer are shrinking. If young people resort to criminal activity in the absence of legitimate opportunities for success, according to traditional anomie theory (Merton, 1938), they can also turn to legitimate jobs in response to dwindling opportunities for illegitimate work (see Freeman, 1996).

Inner-city youth may have responded to opportunities to make money in the drug markets of the late twentieth century, but they did not create those opportunities. Organized crime and state policy-makers set the stage for the involvement of youth in the drug trade and the rise of youth violence. Street-level drug dealers were merely the retail sales force of an enormous and highly differentiated international illicit drug industry. The disadvantaged young street sellers did not cultivate the coca leaves, process them into cocaine, or smuggle the drug into the United States – although their South and Central American counterparts may have. Even relatively organized and sophisticated drug-selling operations such as that run by Detroit's Chambers Brothers occupied, at best, the middle rungs of the industry. For their part, the organized crime groups that dominated the illicit drug industry of the 1980s, such as the Columbian Cali and Medellín cartels, merely exploited opportunities made available to them by the demand for psychoactive drugs and government policies that forced consumers into the underground market to purchase them.

The United States has pursued two basic policies to enforce drug prohibition in the contemporary era. The first, an *interdiction* policy, presses the governments of drug-producing nations to eliminate the drugs and the organizations that supply them at the source. The second, a *deterrence* policy, has vastly increased the legal penalties for drug possession and trafficking in the United States itself. Neither policy has greatly reduced either the supply or the demand for illicit drugs, and both have been linked to escalating rates of violence.

In 1982 the United States sent $2.8 million to Colombia to combat the production and trafficking of illicit drugs. By 1994, US assistance had risen to $26 million and then to $800 million by the end of the Clinton presidency, making Colombia the largest recipient of US aid after Israel and Egypt (Crandall, 2008: 1). Although cocaine production in Colombia fell as US assistance increased during the period, levels of violence skyrocketed, eventually including the assassinations of one-third of the Colombian Supreme Court, 'at least 60 lower court justices, the nation's Justice Minister, several presidential candidates, and hundreds of police officers and prosecutors' (Kenney and Finckenauer, 1995: 194). Meanwhile, the street price of cocaine in the United States fell as production, trafficking routes, and the violence associated with the drug trade were displaced to other South and Central American nations, notably Mexico. In early 2012, Mexican authorities reported 47,515 drug-related killings in that nation since President Felipe Calderón declared war on the drug cartels in 2006 (*New York Times*, 2012a).

The death toll in the United States connected to the illicit drug trade never approached these catastrophic levels or threatened state security, but it too can be linked to escalated enforcement of over-regulation policies. On the domestic front, the war on drugs fuelled a dramatic spike in imprisonment for drug offences. In 1980, 19,000 persons were serving prison sentences in the United States for drug offences; by 2005 the figure had risen to 253,000, a 1,233% increase. By comparison, over the same period, persons imprisoned for violent and property crimes rose by 297% and 179%, respectively.[9] As adult drug dealers were taken off the streets, they were replaced by adolescents and younger adults whose reduced legal liability and willingness to take risks stoked the increase in youth violence beginning in the 1980s (Blumstein, 1995). Yet, there would have been few opportunities for the youthful drug sellers of the 1980s – or the bootleggers and racketeers of the 1920s – had state policy not offered a profitable niche for organized crime to supply and market a product that consumers wanted. When over-regulation policies and their enforcement do not greatly diminish the demand for illicit commodities, they risk promoting the very harms they are intended to control.

Under-regulation, the housing crisis, and white-collar crime

The physical embodiment of the 'American dream' is the single-family home. No other material or symbolic emblem commands as much public or policy support. All American tax-payers are eligible to deduct the interest paid on their home mortgages; most renters receive no comparable government assistance. Massive federal programmes, such as the guaranteed loan programmes of the Federal Housing Administration,

---

[9] Prisoner statistics are from the Bureau of Justice Statistics (http://bjs.ojp.usdoj.gov/index.cfm?ty=tp&tid=1).

lower the costs of home-ownership for families of modest means. Although home-ownership rates in the United States are not notably higher than those in other developed industrial nations and even many developing nations, it is difficult to underestimate the cultural significance of the single family home for Americans. Owning a home remains the lynchpin of the American success ethic.[10]

The housing crisis that began in 2008 was a direct assault on the American dream. Four million families lost their homes to foreclosure between 2007 and early 2012 (*New York Times*, 2012b). The question that remains unsettled as we write is the extent to which the foreclosure crisis involved criminal activity by lenders, although investigations into the possibility of criminal prosecutions have commenced at the state and federal level. One lending practice was clearly illegal, the practice of 'robo-signing' home loans by lenders who had not actually reviewed them. But what of other practices that characterized and to a large degree brought about the housing crisis, such as the packaging of multiple subprime mortgage loans in exotic financial instruments like 'credit default swaps' that were sold (and resold) at hugely inflated prices? These innovative financial practices were not illegal, although many would have been a quarter of a century earlier prior to the deregulation of the banking industry. But they proved to be catastrophic to home-owners and financial firms alike once the housing bubble burst, home prices tumbled, borrowers defaulted on their loans, the financial system teetered on the brink of collapse, and tax-payers were called on to clean up the mess.

If not crimes, per se, how should we view such plainly destructive business practices? They can be regarded as 'crime equivalents', that is, technically legal behaviours that cause individual and social harms comparable to those of serious crimes. White-collar crime analysts Henry Pontell and William Black refer to the lending practices that drove the housing bubble of the early twenty-first century as 'control frauds', accounting methods deployed as 'weapons' by ostensibly legitimate firms to defraud their customers and competitors (Black, 2010;

---

[10] International home-ownership rates are from the European Mortgage Federation (2009). On the continuing significance of home-ownership in the United States, see Brennan (2011).

Nguyen and Pontell, 2010; Pontell and Black, 2012). According to these authors, the key to understanding the genesis and epidemic-like spread of the recent housing and financial crises, and the crimes and crime-equivalents that fuelled them, is the absence of effective regulation. As Black (2010: 617) has noted: 'The current crisis was not contained because financial non-regulation was the norm, which created a criminogenic environment.'

The story of the housing and financial crises that engulfed the United States and much of Europe in the first decade of the twenty-first century combines the three powerful themes of our discussion of the illicit drug market: consumer demand, government regulation, and criminal opportunity. But, in the case of the housing and financial crises, the problem was not too *much* regulation, but too *little*. Further, the opportunities for profit afforded by the regulatory environment were exploited by some of the most trusted and venerable financial firms – Bear Stearns, Lehman Brothers, Citigroup, Bank of America – not criminal gangs and racketeers. Finally, the over-regulation policies that generated the market in illicit drugs did not create the demand for mind-altering substances (except, perhaps, through the lure of forbidden fruit). The demand for single-family homes, however, was underwritten by government policies that enabled millions of consumers to purchase homes they otherwise would not have been able to afford – especially as average income stagnated while house prices shot up prior to the housing crisis and near collapse of the financial system in 2008.

The regulatory framework of the modern banking system in the United States was created during the Great Depression and remained essentially unchanged for the next half century. The cornerstone of banking regulation was the Glass-Steagall Act, passed by Congress in 1933 at the height of the economic crisis. Glass-Steagall placed limits on the interest rates banks could offer on deposits, established the Federal Deposit Insurance Corporation (FDIC) that guaranteed consumer deposits, and prohibited banks from being '"engaged principally" in non-banking activities, such as the securities or insurance business' (Sherman, 2009: 4). The result was a staid and stable financial system that lasted until the latter part of the century, when banking underwent significant deregulation.

In the 1980s and 1990s the Federal Reserve loosened the restrictions on the involvement of banks in the securities and insurance business. In 1999, Congress repealed Glass-Steagall as part of the Financial Modernization Act, which one observer called a 'monumental piece of deregulation' that was the 'crowning achievement of decades and millions of dollars worth of lobbying efforts on behalf of the finance industry' (Sherman, 2009: 10). Deregulation led to the creation of 'mega-banks' that combined traditional banking with investment firms, facilitated the trade in 'complex and opaque' financial instruments such as credit default swaps and collateralized debt obligations (Simkovic, 2009), and fuelled the over-leveraging and housing bubble that culminated in the financial crisis of 2008 (Sherman, 2009).

Few of the big players in the events leading to the financial crisis foresaw the disastrous outcomes of their actions. Merton (1936) described several factors that give rise to the unanticipated consequences of purposive social action, including ignorance, error, and values. The factor most pertinent to the current discussion is what Merton called the 'imperious immediacy of interest', whereby 'the actor's paramount concern with the foreseen immediate consequences excludes the consideration of further or other consequences of the same act'. Anticipating later treatments of cognitive bias in market behaviour (e.g., Kahneman, 2011), Merton held that 'strong concern with the satisfaction of the immediate interest is a psychological generator of emotional bias, with consequent lopsidedness or failure to engage in the required calculations' (Merton, 1936: 901–2). Biased thinking of this sort certainly motivated the behaviour of many actors who sought quick gains from the run up in housing prices prior to the financial crisis, including millions of home-buyers who took on mortgage debt they could not afford.

Curbing the unanticipated consequences of cognitive bias is a chief purpose of financial regulation, indeed, of the regulation of market activity of all kinds. Regulation, to be sure, may reduce market efficiency, but often that is just what it is supposed to do. As the psychologist Barry Schwartz (2012: 9) has pointed out, 'too much efficiency – too little friction – might be a bad thing'. It is more efficient, for example, to bundle dozens or hundreds of mortgages into securities than to spend the time and money required to check the creditworthiness of each individual loan applicant. By introducing 'friction' into market transactions, regulation can reduce the bias of immediate interest and enable 'both institutions and individuals to make better decisions' (Schwartz, 2012: 9).

The crimes and crime-equivalents that accompanied the financial crisis, in summary, resulted from under-regulation policies that removed restraints on the free flow of finance capital and created incentives for financial innovation and opportunities for lenders and investors to more efficiently exploit the demand for home-ownership. But, to paraphrase Schwartz (2012), too much regulation may also be a bad thing. As we have seen, over-regulation in the face of high consumer demand may generate underground markets in illicit commodities where violence is deployed as a means of social control. The policy challenge, then, is to devise regulations that minimize incentives and opportunities for irresponsible, reckless, and bias-ridden market behaviour without driving markets underground or stifling the creativity, dynamism, efficiencies, and performance of market economies. We address this issue in the following chapter, but promise no grand solution to a conundrum that has bedevilled thoughtful analysts and policy-makers from Adam Smith, to John Maynard Keynes, to Paul Volker (Uchitelle, 2010).

To make matters more complicated, even carefully calibrated regulations are no panacea for market-generated crime. At best, market regulation improves long-run economic performance and reduces opportunities for organized and white-collar crime. Effective monetary and fiscal policy may also reduce the demand for stolen goods and the street crimes that ebb and flow in tandem with the rhythms of market economies. But, as we have suggested, criminal motivations are generated, and restraints against crime are enfeebled, by the very structure of the market economy when it dominates the institutional order of a society and vitiates non-economic values, controls, and supports. Better regulation of commodity markets will not solve this problem, which requires nothing less than the realignment of social institutions.

FIVE

implications for policy and social change

In the introduction to Chapter 2, we called attention to the virtue of *theory* in any scientific discipline. We quoted Carl Hempel, a renowned philosopher of science, who observed that sound theories provide us with 'a deeper and more accurate understanding of the phenomena in question' (Hempel, 1966: 70). The overarching objective of Chapter 4 was to make the case that an 'institutional perspective' on crime does precisely that; it deepens our understanding of crime in advanced capitalist societies.

In this chapter, we explore the implications of our theoretical frame-work for social policy and social change.[1] Members of the general public and scholars alike are interested not only in understanding crime, but also in using theoretical knowledge to guide actions that could potentially enhance personal safety by reducing the risks of criminal victimization. Social scientists have long recognized the importance of converting theoretical knowledge into practical strategies for the benefit of society. This principle was perhaps stated most eloquently by Karl Marx. In a very famous and widely cited passage, Marx wrote: 'The philosophers have only *interpreted* the world in various ways; the point is to *change* it' (Feuer, 1959: 245; original emphasis).

When considering the implications of our arguments for reducing crime in the advanced industrial nations, it is tempting to identify the 'culprits' that generate crime (e.g., weak individual or social controls, economic downturns, over- or under-regulation, institutional imbalance)

---

[1] Portions of this chapter are adapted from Rosenfeld and Messner (2010).

and simply propose that alterations in those traits or conditions will result in less crime. We resist that temptation, in part because it is politically naïve but also because the ensuing policy recommendations are likely to be intellectually facile. We have argued throughout this book that the economic causes of crime are not simple or straightforward. They may be mediated or moderated by conditions that are poorly understood or are resistant to change. They may differ for different types of crime. And, most importantly, they may be part of broader cultural or social forces that few people would want to change – even if they believe such conditions constitute the 'root causes' of crime. Modesty is the best policy in any discussion of crime reduction.

Our discussion is organized around four key issues that should be addressed when considering the implications of the arguments and evidence for crime reduction presented in this book. The first issue involves the complex connection between social policy and social change. The second concerns the distinction between 'proximate' and 'ultimate' causes and its relevance for crime-control policy. The third issue we consider concerns the limits of individual-level interventions to reduce crime. Finally, we discuss the implications for policy and social change of an institutional perspective on the connection between the economy and crime.

Policy versus social change: the costs of mass incarceration

'Policy', as generally understood, refers to modifications in the means by which predetermined ends are accomplished; rarely does policy seek to alter the fundamental ends or purposes of a society. For example, Marxist critiques of the British welfare state during the 1970s, which called for abolishing capitalism, were widely regarded as beyond the pale of realistic policy debate (Blakemore and Griggs, 2007). Basic transformations in the economic and social organization of a society are a consequence of social change. Social change transfers power from one group to another, generates new ways of producing and distributing goods and services, or elevates some groups in a society's prestige hierarchy and demotes others. By contrast, policy, when effective, typically improves the means by which existing collective goals are attained. An example of social change discussed in this book is Russia's transition from a socialist to a proto-capitalist political economy after the fall of the Soviet Union. An example of policy change is the deregulation of the banking industry in the United States during the 1980s and 1990s which was intended to improve the efficiency of financial markets.

On occasion, however, policies emerge from and are designed to implement social change. Examples include the anti-discrimination policies resulting from the civil rights and women's movements during the 1960s and 1970s, and legislation guaranteeing workers' collective bargaining rights passed during the Great Depression of the 1930s. Such policies alter social goals regarding fundamental rights and liberties and not merely the means of realizing pre-established goals.[2] We might term them 'policies with change' and distinguish them from 'policies without change'. An instructive example of policy without change is the suite of sentencing reforms that produced the era of mass incarceration in the United States.

During the 1970s several criminologists sought to explain the remarkable temporal stability in imprisonment rates in the United States and other nations with reference to Durkheim's idea that societies stabilize levels of crime and punishment to maintain social solidarity (Blumstein and Cohen, 1973; Blumstein et al., 1976). No sooner had the 'stability of punishment' hypothesis been advanced, prison populations in the United States began climbing to historically unprecedented levels. Imprisonment rates increased five-fold from the mid-1970s to 2010 (Guerino et al., 2011; Rosenfeld and Messner, 2010). So much for the stability of punishment in the United States at the end of the twentieth century.

A classic statement in the sociology of punishment links the size of the prison population to changes in the labour market (Rusche and Kirchheimer, 2003 [1939]). According to this argument, prisons function to regulate the supply of labour in capitalist societies. When labour is in short supply and unemployment rates are low, pressures mount to

---

[2] On the other hand, civil rights policies can be viewed as extending the pre-existing goal of equal opportunity to all citizens rather than establishing new political goals.

reduce the size of the prison population. When labour markets are slack and unemployment rises, the prison population expands. Research on the labour supply hypothesis has returned mixed results, at best.[3] And how can it account for the era of mass incarceration in the United States, when imprisonment rates shot up five-fold with no apparent connection to oscillating unemployment rates during the same period?

Interpreted broadly, however, Rusche and Kirchheimer's argument does help to explain the historical relationship between punishment policy and the political economy of the United States. 'Wherever you look in the development of modernist penality you will find labour', according to Jonathan Simon (1993: 39). As the American economy has undergone structural change, from the rise of the factory system in the nineteenth century to the decline in the demand for unskilled factory labour in the latter part of the twentieth century, the policy and practice of 'corrections', as it is still quaintly called, have adapted accordingly. Mass incarceration, according to Simon (1993) and other analysts (e.g., Garland, 2001; Gottschalk, 2006; Western, 2006) arose in part as a response to the concomitant expansion of the urban underclass in the 1970s and 1980s (Wilson, 1987). Chronically high levels of joblessness in US inner cities, growing family disruption, and community disorder and decline, prompted policy-makers to search for substitute means of social control. 'In a very real sense,' Elliott Currie (2012: 46) has written, 'our swollen prison system has functioned as a costly and ineffective alternative to serious efforts to address those enduring social deficits'.

Mass incarceration is not a discrete policy, but the result of several policies intended to 'get tough' on crime and illegal drugs (Messner and Rosenfeld, 2007a: 115–18). It is fair to assume that few policy-makers intended or foresaw a quintupling of the prison population as a consequence of the mandatory-minimum sentencing and truth-in-sentencing laws passed over the last 35 years, but once the dramatic escalation in incarceration became evident, if policy-makers were inclined to limit future imprisonment growth, presumably they would have done so by now (Tonry, 1996, 2004).

---

[3] See the reviews in Garland (1990) and Melosi's introduction to Rusche and Kirchheimer (2003 [1939]).

One reason for the reluctance of policy-makers to substantially alter sentencing policies is the assumption that imprisonment growth has reduced crime. To understand the impact of imprisonment on crime, it is useful to recall the distinction between criminal motivations and criminal opportunities. Criminal motivations refer to the desire or propensity of individuals to engage in criminal behaviour. Criminal opportunities are the situational inducements (e.g., an unlocked door, an open window, lack of surveillance) and impediments (e.g., locks, barriers, guards) that make crime more or less easy to commit. Persons with little or no criminal motivation are unlikely to commit crime regardless of the opportunity to do so. But even highly motivated would-be offenders may refrain from criminal behaviour if adequate criminal opportunities are absent. For criminality to give rise to criminal acts, in other words, some opportunity to commit crime must exist. Imprisonment is a potent method for suppressing criminal acts by denying incarcerated offenders the opportunity to commit crimes against the general public. Criminologists term the reduction of criminal opportunities through imprisonment the 'incapacitation effect' of incarceration.

In principle, incarceration not only suppresses crime by incapacitating offenders but also by deterring prisoners from committing crimes after they are released, which is termed 'specific' deterrence, or by deterring others from committing crimes through the threat of imprisonment, termed 'general' deterrence. Whether incarceration has much of a deterrent effect on criminal behaviour, either specific or general, remains uncertain (see Durlauf and Nagin, 2011; Nagin, 1998). Few criminologists believe that imprisonment as currently constituted in the United States reduces crime by rehabilitating criminal offenders, that is, by reducing criminal motivations.[4] But the incapacitation effects of imprisonment growth in the United States over the past several decades are beyond dispute, even if the magnitude of those effects is subject to debate (DeFina and Arvanites, 2002; Levitt, 1996; Rosenfeld and Fornango, 2007; Spelman, 2006; Western, 2006).

---

[4] John Braithwaite (1989) has argued that imprisonment policies such as those practiced in the United States are likely to fail because they are predicated upon 'stigmatizing shaming'. Braithwaite proposes that policies based on a philosophy of 'reintegrative shaming' are likely to be more effective at fostering rehabilitation and reducing recidivism.

Mass incarceration is an example of a broader class of policy initiatives that seek to influence some social outcome – in this case crime rates – without fundamentally changing the cultural and social conditions that generate that outcome. As a policy without change, mass incarceration does not represent new goals for criminal justice but revised means for achieving the traditional goals of crime control and criminal justice: keeping dangerous people off the streets and punishing them for their misdeeds. Mandatory-minimum sentences and truth-in-sentencing laws reduce the discretion of judges and corrections officials in setting criminal sentences and releasing inmates from prison, thereby insuring that larger numbers of convicted offenders are imprisoned for longer periods of time. These changes strengthen the hand of prosecutors at the expense of the discretionary authority traditionally granted judges and corrections managers in the sentencing process, but they do not alter the basic character or goals of criminal sentencing or related institutional practices.

Mass incarceration is a stopgap policy for reducing crime – by how much and for how long remains uncertain – without having to change the conditions that produce or strengthen criminal motivations. Pursuing crime control largely through incarceration is akin to managing illness and disease through hospitalization without treating the underlying medical conditions that make people sick. A rich society could continue storing the sick in hospitals for a long time, but at tremendous cost and diminishing benefits.

We should expect policies that in effect substitute for, rather than implement, social change to exact a high price in economic, political, and social capital. The economic costs of mass incarceration can be reckoned in two ways: first, by the amount of money spent to build the jails and prisons and hire the staff needed to guard the growing number of prisoners, and second, by what economists term the 'opportunity' costs of these outlays, that is, what we might have done with the money had we not spent it on prison expansion. Expenditure on corrections in the United States increased to $74.2 billion in 2007 from $21.4 billion in 1982, or by 247%, in 2007 constant dollars. Local, state, and federal expenditures for legal and judicial services added another $49.7 billion to criminal justice outlays in 2007 (Kyckelhahn, 2011: Table 2).

The United States is a rich nation and can afford to maintain a huge corrections complex, even though mounting correction expenditures have far outstripped overall growth in the US economy. But correction costs are borne primarily by state and local governments, and they have grown at roughly double the rate of state and local outlays for education, health care, and policing over the past 30 years (Hughes, 2006). Each additional dollar spent on prisons, jails, and community corrections is money that states and local areas cannot devote to other pressing needs, including improvements in education and early childhood interventions that hold some promise for reducing criminal motivations, and not just containing crime rates (Greenwood et al., 1998).[5]

As costly as mass incarceration in the United States is in purely economic terms, it also has significant political and social costs that researchers have only recently begun to analyze in depth, including destabilizing effects on families and communities, a growing population of permanently disenfranchised ex-prisoners and other convicted felons, and, quite possibly, higher crime rates over the long term (Liedka et al., 2006; Manza and Uggen, 2006; Pager, 2007; Pattillo et al., 2004; Travis and Visher, 2005). Moreover, the costs of mass incarceration are not spread evenly across the population but are borne disproportionately by African-Americans. More than 3% of black males in the United States were serving time in a state or federal prison in 2010 compared to 1.3% of Hispanic males and 0.5% of white males (Guerino et al., 2011: Appendix, Table 14). Arrest rates for many serious offences are also higher among African-Americans than other groups, but only a small part of the growth in incarceration over the past three decades has resulted from a rise in crime. Most of the growth is from changes in sentencing and recommitment policies that, whether intentionally or not, have disproportionately affected the life chances of African-Americans (Blumstein and Beck, 2005; Tonry, 1996).

In summary, the US case indicates that the costs of mass incarceration are likely to be high, difficult to control, multifarious, and unequally distributed across the population. A natural question is whether the costs of a policy equal or exceed the benefits. This question proves

---

[5] See CrimeSolutions.gov for assessments of the effectiveness of crime reduction programmes.

to be a very difficult one to answer in the case of mass incarceration. For one thing, the magnitude and duration of the effects of imprisonment growth on crime remain uncertain. But more importantly, it is far from clear how we should weigh the benefits of less crime against the escalating costs of mass incarceration. How much are we willing to increase community instability or voter disenfranchisement to avert one additional robbery or burglary (or ten or 100) through increased incarceration? How much less should we spend on education or healthcare to avert an additional homicide? The costs and (possible) benefits of mass incarceration simply do not share a common metric against which such tradeoffs can be reconciled.

It should be apparent that simply adding up the economic losses from crime (medical expenses, time lost from work, etc.) and comparing them with the economic costs of imprisonment does not capture the full range of costs associated with either crime or incarceration. Nor is it clear how economists' efforts to fully 'monetize' the costs of crime (i.e., assign a dollar value to all costs, no matter how intangible) can help policy-makers and informed citizens make the difficult political and moral tradeoffs inherent in deciding how many people to incarcerate to lower the crime rate.[6]

It is nevertheless useful to consider whether many of the purported benefits of mass incarceration can be attained through alternative means. Can we achieve whatever crime reductions are attributable to mass incarceration by implementing programmes and policies that are less costly to the public purse, the affected families and communities (of both offenders and victims), and a democratic polity? Two policy analysts who have studied crime control in the United States have held that both imprisonment and crime can be reduced by transferring resources currently devoted to prisons to expanding policing strategies of proven effectiveness (Durlauf and Nagin, 2011). Despite the obstacles associated with moving budget expenditures from one level of government to another – as noted, prisons are largely a state responsibility in the United States, while the costs of policing are borne mainly by local governments – in principle there is much to recommend such a policy shift. Carefully targeting enforcement strategies at crime 'hot

_____
[6] See Cohen (2005) on monetizing the costs of crime and criminal justice.

spots' has been shown to reduce crime and not merely shift it to other areas (Braga and Weisburd, 2010). But, like incarceration, targeted policing simply reduces criminal opportunities; substantial and enduring crime reduction will require public policies that address the motivations and not just the opportunities to commit crime.

Opportunities as proximate causes of crime

The historian Randolph Roth (2009) has criticized contemporary criminology for focusing too heavily on the proximate causes of crime to the neglect of the ultimate causes. In his study of the history of homicide in the United States, Roth (2009) rejects most of the presumed causes of homicide dear to the hearts of criminologists, including drugs, guns, inequality, poverty, unemployment, and deterrence. These and like factors are not necessarily irrelevant to the study of homicide, but they do not fully explain it. They are, at most, proximate causes that are associated with homicide at particular times and places, but they are not ultimate causes that stand the test of time (Rosenfeld, 2011b).[7]

Criminal opportunities, in our view, are best thought of as proximate causes of crime, characteristics of the immediate situation or milieu that trigger or restrain criminal acts. Criminal motivations and the conditions that stimulate them are closer to ultimate causes: they reside deeper in the social structure and are implicated in a society's basic values and beliefs. Criminal opportunities by their very nature are more ephemeral and subject to situational variation; that is one reason they are more amenable than criminal motivations to policy manipulation, such as the move to targeted patrols and other forms of 'smart policing'. That does not make crime prevention through opportunity reduction ineffective, at least in the short run, but it does raise questions about the scope and penetration of social control entailed in eliminating opportunities for crime.

---

[7] The distinction between proximate and ultimate causes is well developed in the study of animal behaviour. See Diamond (1992) for a readable discussion and numerous examples.

Opportunity reduction often involves restrictions on freedom of movement and other everyday liberties, as anyone who has travelled by air over the past decade can attest. In the United States, young minority males who are routinely stopped and questioned by the police pay an especially high price for the benefits of at least some versions of targeted policing (Peart, 2011). Omnipresent barriers, gates, grates, alarms, cameras, screening and tracking technologies, and security personnel represent the extension of the disciplinary principles and devices of the prison to public life in the contemporary city (Marx, 1985; Parenti, 2003).[8] Ameliorating the deep-seated structural and cultural sources of criminal motivation may actually prove less invasive than seeking to eliminate criminal opportunities through a thousand cuts to individual freedoms and democratic values.

Policies that address the ultimate causes of crime are also likely to have more enduring consequences than those that modify the more proximate catalysts of criminal activity. Consider the impact of the normal rhythms of market economies on crime, discussed in the previous chapter, in relation to the crime declines in the United States and Europe during the 1990s. The crime drop did not result from fundamental changes in prevailing social conditions in the developed Western world. Social institutions did not become notably more controlling or supportive during the last decade of the twentieth century. In fact, with the end of 'welfare as we know it' in the United States and the spread of neoliberal economic and social policies throughout Europe, the developed nations had become less supportive of the poor (Prasad, 2006). Rather, the crime drop coincided with the expansion of the Western economies during the 1990s (see Rosenfeld and Messner, 2009). There is good reason to expect that the booming economy contributed to the crime drop, not simply because of the scale of the 1990s economic expansion, but because, as shown in Chapter 4, crime rates typically respond to the periodic fluctuations that characterize dynamic market economies. When the economy expands, crime rates tend to fall, and when the economy contracts, crime rates tend to rise. If the

_____

[8] See Huang and Low (2008) for a discussion of the boom of gated housing construction in contemporary urban China, and for a comparison of gated communities in US and Chinese cities.

1990s crime drop was steeper than previous crime reductions, that was in part because it was driven by the longest peacetime economic expansion on record.

The normal rhythms of market economies constitute proximate causes of crime because they are contained within the structure and regulatory capacity of existing economic and social institutions. They neither reflect nor produce significant alterations in the moral order of capitalist society. The monetary and fiscal policies intended to improve the performance of the economy are policies without change that, when effective, expand economic opportunities by reducing unemployment and increasing incomes. 'Opportunities', in this context, refer to the possibilities for social and economic mobility in a society and not to the situational inducements and impediments to crime we have been discussing. But the two criminological meanings of the term share an important feature in common: both imply crime reduction without institutional regulation.

Recall that institutional regulation directs attention to the *moral* bases of conformity to norms. When the regulatory force of norms is strong, people conform out of a sense of duty, obligation, and judgements of right and wrong. Under such conditions a relatively strong 'moral filter' tends to effectively exclude crimes from the realm of behavioural alternatives.[9] When norms lose their regulatory authority, people may still conform but their willingness to do so results primarily from a calculative, utilitarian evaluation of the costs and benefits of alternative courses of action. At the extreme, an anomic cultural environment encourages people to pursue their goals 'by any means necessary'. Behaviour is governed strictly by what the sociologist Robert Merton called 'efficiency norms'; people select means for attaining goals that are technically expedient without regard to their normative status.

As the institutional regulation of behaviour weakens, conformity and deviance become ever more dependent on institutional performance. When the economy is booming, legitimate means for pursuing goals

---

[9] Wikström's situational-action theory highlights the ways in which the 'moral filter' inhibits crime by restricting the 'action alternatives' that a person considers (see Wikström, 2010, 2011). Messner (2012) discusses points of convergence between situational-action theory, a micro-level criminological theory, and institutional-anomie theory, the macro-level criminological theory we introduced in Chapter 3.

are more widely available, and criminal behaviour becomes less attractive from a purely calculative, tactical standpoint. Conversely, when the economy contracts, access to the legitimate means is restricted and the technical superiority of the illegitimate means increases. Regardless of whether the focus is on the restriction of criminal opportunities or on the expansion of mobility opportunities, the manipulation of opportunities is the only policy option available under conditions of weak institutional regulation. When institutional regulation is strong, by contrast, institutional performance should matter less in the moral deliberation to commit a crime, and crime rates should depend less on fluctuating opportunities.

In summary, policies and programmes intended to increase the costs of crime by reducing criminal opportunities may exact a high price in societies that value individual freedom. Those that increase the benefits of conformity by expanding mobility opportunities are subject to the normal swings in the performance of a capitalist economy. Either way, measures directed solely at manipulating opportunities to reduce crime are likely to encounter significant limits to their effectiveness over the long run because they fail to address the market dynamics of the demand for crime.

Levels of analysis and illegal markets

Throughout its brief history, criminology has swung back and forth between an emphasis on explaining individual criminal behaviour and explaining patterns and trends in crime rates.[10] But the pendulum never swings too far, especially in American criminology, from a preoccupation with individual criminality and the micro environments (families, schools, neighbourhoods) in which its putative causes are located. The current period, with its breakthrough studies of gene–environment interactions and individual development, epitomizes the dominance of micro criminology.

If individual-level analysis holds sway in criminology today, it is also true that allusions to aggregate crime rates abound in current research,

---

[10] This section draws on material in Rosenfeld (2011b).

including studies of individual criminal and antisocial behaviour. Individual-level studies often open with a statement that hooks the research to a critical public problem, almost always unacceptably high levels of serious crime. After that, however, the 'big picture' of aggregate crime disappears. For example, a review of research on gene–environment interaction in the production of antisocial behaviour begins as follows: 'Despite assiduous efforts to eliminate it, antisocial behaviour is still a problem. Approximately 20% of people in the developed world experience victimization by perpetrators of violent and non-violent illegal behaviour each year ...' (Moffitt, 2005: 533). A paper on violent behaviour in children and adolescents begins similarly:

> Juvenile aggression and violence affect society in a wide and penetrating manner. The victimization and the distress caused by these behaviours are staggering; the numbers of perpetrators and victims have gradually increased over the past decades ... (Loeber and Stouthamer-Loeber, 1998: 242).

Each paper proceeds to describe research on the factors that distinguish antisocial individuals from others, but neither returns to the opening sentences on crime in populations and explains how better research of the kind under consideration, and the policies based on it, would reduce aggregate crime rates. The strong implication is that no such explanation is needed. But the link between individual differences in antisocial behaviour and the crime rates of whole societies is not obvious and, as far as we know, has never been demonstrated. A hypothetical scenario is helpful for thinking through the steps needed to forge the connection.

Suppose we had a pill that, when administered to highly antisocial children, reduced their subsequent crimes by 20% from the level expected without the treatment. Suppose, further, that these children constitute 5% of all future offenders and, if untreated, would go on to commit 50% of future crimes. All else being equal, the reduction in crimes attributable to the treatment would be 10%.[11] That is a sizable impact and the assumptions informing this thought experiment – a 20%

---

[11] If the treatment reduces future crimes by 20% and is administered to those children who would have committed 50% of the crimes, then the impact of the treatment is 10% ((.20 x .50) x 100).

effect size, 5% of offenders committing 50% of the crimes – are in line with research on the effectiveness of the best early interventions and the pronounced skew in the commission of serious crime. This seems to be the kind of logic that, if explicated, underlies the implied connection between reducing the criminal propensities of individuals and reducing the aggregate crime rate. Now let us see what this logic assumes away.

Crime is a function of both supply and demand factors, as discussed in Chapter 4. Studies of individual differences in criminal behaviour focus almost exclusively on the supply side. The policy implication seems to be that reductions in the supply of offenders will lead ipso facto to reductions in crime. This policy logic assumes away the demand for crime. But market-oriented crimes, which constitute the great majority of all serious crimes in advanced capitalist societies, are committed in response to consumer demand for the goods or services criminals provide. Now, if the prosocial pill in our scenario were successful in reducing the current supply of criminal offenders, what would happen to the market for crime? A drop in supply should increase the price of illegal goods and services. As a result, demand might fall as well, but incentives for new suppliers to enter the market would increase, given the higher returns of crime. Depending on the elasticity of demand[12] and the strength of price incentives, the initial reduction in the supply of offenders might or might not result in a decrease in the rate of market-oriented crime (Bushway and Reuter, 2011). Given the dynamic interplay of supply and demand forces in illegal markets, however, it is virtually certain that reducing the supply of criminal offenders will not produce a one-to-one drop in market crimes in the long run.

This market analysis of crime, which Bushway and Reuter (2011) use to question the effectiveness of deterrence strategies in decreasing drug crimes, applies in principle to all crimes committed in response to consumer demand, which includes most property crimes, violent crimes such as robbery, and personal-service crimes such as prostitution, in addition to drug-selling. Furthermore, market analysis can be usefully applied to any crime-reduction strategy, including early interventions to improve family functioning (Welsh and Piquero, 2011), which

---

[12] The 'elasticity of demand' is the term economists use to describe the responsiveness of demand for a good or service to its price.

focuses solely on diminishing the supply of criminal offenders without taking into account the demand for crime.

Two key questions about the efficacy of our hypothetical treatment for antisocial behaviour, or any policy or programme that focuses prevention efforts on individuals at highest risk for criminal offending, are (1) whether the treatment will staunch the flow of new entrants to the criminal marketplace, and (2) whether the treatment will reduce the demand for crime. With respect to the first question, the treatment might be very effective when administered to those willing to commit crimes at some given level of incentives, but what about those enticed into crime by greater incentives, that is, higher market returns per unit of effort? As Bushway and Reuter (2011) point out, criminal incentives are not constant; they shift up or down according to changing market conditions. Incentives to commit crime should increase as the supply of offenders decreases, as long as consumer demand for illegal goods and services does not fall as rapidly as the supply.

The lure of higher returns for effort will bring into the market offenders unwilling to risk criminal activity with fewer incentives. By definition, these new entrants are more risk averse than those they replace and less likely to fit the inclusion criteria for treatment.[13] We could of course cast the treatment net more widely to capture those with lower tolerance for risk. But their market replacements would be even more risk averse and the treatment net would have to be widened accordingly. The supply of potential offenders is not inexhaustible, but as long as potential offenders differ in their response to incentives and preferences for risk, it will remain a moving target. And as long as the demand for illegal goods and services does not fall as rapidly as the supply of criminals willing and able to provide them, the aggregate rate of crime will remain high in relation to even the most effective treatments that target would-be offenders.

But should we not expect programmes or treatments that effectively reduce the supply of criminal offenders to also cut the demand for crime? After all, those who buy illicit drugs or stolen merchandise are

---

[13] Low-risk aversion is part of most definitions of antisocial personality disorder in adults and conduct disorder in juveniles (see American Psychiatric Association, 2000; Lahey et al., 2003).

also breaking the law. Although it is difficult to tell, this would seem to be part of the implicit logic that connects aggregate crime rates to individual criminal propensities. That logic is subject to the same limitations of supply-side interventions when applied to the demand side of crime, if it is assumed that consumers of illegal goods and services, like the purveyors, differ in their response to incentives and risk preferences. As sellers are removed from the market, some consumers will drop out as prices rise, assuming no change in risk (e.g., the probability of arrest and punishment for possessing illicit drugs or receiving stolen goods). But as additional sellers are attracted into the market by higher returns, prices should stabilize or fall, increasing incentives for additional consumers to enter the market and putting upward pressure on aggregate crime rates.

In sum, the same market mechanisms that limit the impact on aggregate crime rates of interventions that, in effect, target the supply side of illegal markets are also likely to limit the impact of such interventions on the demand side. But there is an important difference between the suppliers and consumers of illegal goods and services that raises additional questions about the effectiveness of interventions that focus on current or future serious offenders. The consumers are far less likely to be serious offenders than the suppliers.

Even allowing for some overlap between the two populations, there are many more consumers of illegal goods and services than the drug dealers, prostitutes, robbers, burglars, and thieves who supply the illegal markets. It follows that the consumers are more heterogeneous with respect to the early life or more proximate risk factors for serious criminality and, therefore, on the whole are less likely to be targeted by interventions that focus on poor parenting, educational or cognitive deficits, conduct disorder, gang involvement, or antisocial behaviour. Further, consumers of illegal goods and services face lower risks of apprehension and punishment than do the suppliers. Drug-selling is riskier than drug possession; selling sex is riskier than frequenting prostitutes. The large size, considerable heterogeneity, and low risk that characterize the population of consumers of illegal goods and services place further drags on any demand reduction that can be accomplished by interventions which target serious offenders in the hopes of reducing aggregate crime rates.

In short, a market analysis of crime raises significant questions about the connection commonly assumed in micro criminology between reducing individual differences in criminal behaviour and reducing aggregate crime rates. We have extended the market analysis of crime well beyond the market for illicit drugs, where economists have concentrated their attention, to encompass most property crimes, personal-service crimes, and acquisitive violent offences such as robbery. But does this analysis extend to other violent crimes? Serious violent offending is arguably the chief concern of psychologists and criminologists who study antisocial behaviour and its early-life antecedents. Even if our hypothetical treatment for antisocial behaviour might not bring down rates of market-oriented crime, should it not lead to reductions in homicides, assaults, or other crimes to which considerations of supply, demand, and price do not apply?

Individual treatments and interventions may well have a greater impact on violent crime than on property crime, but it would be a mistake to assume that violent crime is not also influenced by illegal markets. As we pointed out in the previous chapter, violent crime rates are elevated in social locations where formal, authoritative means of dispute resolution are unavailable, including illegal markets and the underground economies they service. Honour codes arise in such 'stateless' locales that promote or tolerate violent responses to predation, character contests, and disputes over the terms and conditions of illegal transactions (Anderson, 1999; Black, 1993; Cooney, 2009). It is difficult to determine the proportion of homicides and serious assaults that occur in such contexts, but one analysis shows that if only two of every 10,000 robberies, burglaries, and motor vehicle thefts resulted in a homicide, that would account for a sizable fraction of all homicides committed in the United States (Rosenfeld, 2009). Wherever illegal markets remain extensive and vibrant, we should expect aggregate rates of serious violence to remain high, quite apart from even the most successful efforts to prevent individual antisocial behaviour.

We do not mean to dismiss the contributions of micro criminology. The study of individual differences in serious criminal behaviour and the amelioration programmes based on this research are showpieces of contemporary criminology at its best. Our questions and criticisms are directed only at the assumption of a straightforward connection between effective individual-level interventions and reductions in aggregate rates of crime. There are many good reasons, in addition to reducing criminal motivations, for investing in programmes that improve parenting and strengthen prosocial propensities in children. But if the goal is to reduce crime rates, we will have to look beyond such individual-level interventions to macro-level policies that address the institutional sources of crime. The institutional framework presented in this book offers some leads about how to proceed as well as caveats regarding the limits of social change in societies wedded to existing institutional arrangements.

Market economies, institutional regulation, and crime control

Throughout our discussion of the relationship between crime and the economy, we have cautioned readers that there is no single causal thread tying market economies to criminal activity. The nature of the connection varies by the type of crime (e.g., street crime, white-collar crime) and the aspect of the economy (e.g., unemployment, economic growth, inflation) under consideration; mediating and moderating conditions (e.g., social disorganization, criminal subcultures, underground markets); state regulatory schemes (e.g., drug prohibition, deregulation of financial markets); and the degree to which the market economy is embedded in the broader institutional environment. The policy analyst's view of the connection between crime and the economy will also depend on the particular institutional lens that is used. Focusing on the structure of the market economy – the prevailing rules of the economic game – will provide a different picture of credible policy options than will attending to problems of institutional regulation or performance. It is useful to consider the varying policy options of each of these three institutional perspectives on crime and the economy.

Market economies require several preconditions for their effective functioning: people must be motivated to perform economic functions according to considerations of profit and loss; they must be sensitive to variations in the price of goods and services; and in the advanced market economies, they must be willing and able to consume commodities beyond those needed for basic survival. These are among the most important rules of market economies; they are so important, in fact, there is a widespread tendency to assume they are part of human nature itself and not simply the particular motivational requirements of a specific type of economic organization. Ample reason exists to question this ontological assumption – no one is able to observe 'human nature' in pure, unsocialized form, apart from its myriad historical manifestations in society (Gerth and Mills, 1964).

Are there any realistic policy options on the immediate horizon for transforming the structure of the market economies of the highly developed nations? Not really. None is in immediate danger of succumbing to the abrupt social changes that occurred in the former Soviet Union and its client states during the last decades of the twentieth century. The revolutionary varieties of socialism that once captivated protest movements in the developed nations show no signs of reappearing anytime soon. Instead, a resurgence of pro-market, right-wing ideology and activism has taken place in Europe and the United States, buoyed by fears of immigration and economic stagnation (Erixon, 2011; Skocpol and Williamson, 2012). The structure of free-market capitalism appears to be firmly entrenched in the developed nations, and in the foreseeable future all credible policy options for reducing crime will be proposed, debated, and implemented within the limits imposed by that institutional structure.

That leaves the institutionally-minded policy-maker with two broad options for crime control: bolstering the moral bases of law-abiding behaviour by strengthening institutional regulation and improving the performance of existing institutions. As we have suggested, fine-tuning the performance of the market economy is not likely to produce enduring reductions in crime. Nor will enhancing the performance of criminal justice institutions by strengthening the enforcement capacities of the police or expanding the penal principles of surveillance and population control in public life. Policies and practices that reduce opportunities for crime must be part of any comprehensive programme of crime control in the twenty-first century, but they cannot be the only means by which policy-makers who prize democratic values and are mindful of the collateral costs of crime control attempt to maintain order in a just society. Crime-control policy must also seek to replenish the moral bases of social order and criminal justice.

We have argued that the structure of the market economy is highly resistant to change in contemporary developed nations, but that does not mean that market forces must dominate other social institutions, especially to the degree they do in the United States (Messner and Rosenfeld, 2007a). The institutional balance of power varies markedly across developed societies, and a potent counterweight to the market economy in most of them is the modern welfare state. The welfare state is part of the great 'double movement' in the development of modern capitalism that has prevented the market economy from completely remaking other institutions in its own image (Polanyi, 1957 [1944]). And, as we have shown, societies in which extensive social welfare policies shield the most vulnerable members of the population from the full brunt of market forces tend to experience lower levels of serious criminal violence than those with less generous and more restrictive policies (Messner and Rosenfeld, 1997).

The promise of the welfare state for crime control is not simply to compensate for the deficiencies of the market economy by providing for the unmet material needs of a population. Social welfare programmes 'are not just instrumental arrangements; they are also, and in a high degree, expressions of definite moral conceptions' (Rothstein, 1998: 2). The morality of the modern welfare state emphasizes equality, fairness, justice, and solidarity. As such, the welfare state would appear to be ideal social housing for protection against both the material and moral failings of the market economy (cf. Lacey, 2008; Wilkinson and Pickett, 2009).

If this description of the welfare state strikes some readers as curious, that is because the contemporary welfare state has fallen on hard times and has come under attack from, it seems, all sides. Political liberals question the capacity of governments to provide extensive social insurance for citizens in an era of heightened global competition for capital, resources, and markets. Some social observers worry that the welfare state erodes voluntary sources of mutual aid and civic engagement (Wolfe, 1989). But the harshest attack comes from the political right, and it goes right to the moral foundations of the welfare state. From this perspective, the welfare state is inherently unjust because it forcibly transfers wealth from producers to the undeserving; it saps individual initiative by creating a culture of dependency; and it causes more, not less, crime (Murray, 1984). By the end of the twentieth century, the modern welfare state was on the ideological defensive.

As we write in 2012, in the immediate aftermath of the most severe recession since the Great Depression, when several developed nations face the prospect of huge cutbacks in government spending, defence of the welfare state assumes a special urgency. We have argued that simply manipulating criminal opportunities cannot, by itself, generate sizable and sustained crime reductions and, in any event, poses risks to individual freedom and other cherished values. Programmes to instill prosocial attitudes and behaviour in troubled youth, while laudable and important in their own right, do little to diminish the demand for crime. We see no better way to limit crime and promote justice in contemporary developed societies than to reign in the excesses of market economies with policies that guarantee a decent standard of living to all citizens and, by their very nature, reinforce a sense of mutual obligation and collective responsibility. That is the historic promise of the welfare state as part of a vital and responsive democratic polity. No other institution on the world stage today is as likely to soften the impact of the market economy on crime.

We emphasize in closing that our defence of the welfare state is tailored to the specifics of our arguments concerning the institutional sources of crime and its control in advanced, market-capitalist democracies. Rewriting the rules of the market economy, even if that were desirable, does not seem to be a realistic option at present. However, it is important to remember the key insight developed by Karl Polanyi (1957 [1944]) in his classic treatise, *The Great Transformation*. The organization of an economy around market exchange is not a natural and inevitable feature of human society. The market economy that is ubiquitous around the globe today is the product of specific historical conditions. It is virtually certain that fundamentally new institutional arrangements for producing and distributing goods and services will appear at some point in the future, along with as yet unforeseen political and social institutions. As the criminologist Gary LaFree (1998: 151) has observed, the capacity of humans to adapt to changing circumstances by creating novel rules for social organization constitutes the 'genius of institutionalization'.

We make no claims of being able to envision the institutional innovations that might characterize future societies. Nor can we predict the levels and patterns of crime they will produce. We are convinced, however, that a deep and accurate understanding of the future of crime will require a theoretical perspective that assigns high priority to the workings of the economy and its relationship with other institutions.

references

Adler, William M. 1995. *Land of Opportunity: One Family's Quest for the American Dream in the Age of Crack*. New York: Atlantic Monthly Press.

Agnew, Robert. 2006. *Pressured Into Crime: An Overview of General Strain Theory*. New York: Oxford University Press.

Akers, Ronald L. 1998. *Social Learning and Social Structure: A General Theory of Crime and Deviance*. Boston: Northeastern University Press.

Akers, Ronald L., and Gary F. Jensen. 2006. 'The empirical status of the social learning theory of crime and deviance: The past, present, and future'. In Francis T. Cullen, John Paul Wright, and Kristie R. Blevins (eds), *Taking Stock: The Status of Criminological Theory, Advances in Criminological Theory*, Volume 15. New Brunswick, NJ: Transaction.

Allen, Ralph C. 1996. 'Socioeconomic conditions and property crime'. *American Journal of Economics and Sociology*, 55: 293–308.

American Psychiatric Association. 2000. *Diagnostic and Statistical Manual of Mental Disorders DSM-IV-TR*. Fourth edition, text revision. Arlington, VA: American Psychiatric Publishing.

Anderson, Elijah. 1999. *Code of the Street: Decency, Violence, and the Moral Life of the Inner City*. New York: W. W. Norton.

Arvanites, Thomas M., and Robert H. Defina. 2006. 'Business cycles and street crime'. *Criminology*, 44: 139–64.

Associated Press. 2011. 'Amid tough economy, investors hail pawnshops, payday lenders'. *St. Louis Post-Dispatch* (11 July): A8.

Beaver, Kevin M. 2009. *Biosocial Criminology: A Primer*. Dubuque, IA: Kendall/Hunt.

Beaver, Kevin M., and Eric Connolly. 2011. 'Gene-environment interactions and the development of childhood antisocial behavior: Current evidence and directions for future research.' In Chris L. Gibson and Marvin Krohn (eds), *Handbook of Life-Course Criminology*. New York: Springer-Verlag.

Beccaria, Cesare. 1995 [1766]. *On Crimes and Punishments and Other Writings*. New York: Cambridge University Press.

Becker, Gary. 1968. 'Crime and punishment: An economic approach'. *Journal of Political Economy*, 73: 169–217.

Bentham, Jeremy. 1996 [1789]. *An Introduction to the Principles of Morals and Legislation*. Oxford: Clarendon.

Black, Donald J. 1993. *The Social Structure of Right and Wrong*. San Diego, CA: Academic Press.

Black, William K. 2010. 'Echo epidemics: Control frauds generate "white-collar street crime" waves'. *Criminology & Public Policy*, 9: 613–19.

Blakely, Edward J., and Mary Gail Snyder. 1998. 'Separate places: Crime and security in gated communities'. In Marcus Felson and R.B. Peiser (eds), *Reducing Crime Through Real Estate Development and Management*. Washington, DC: Urban Land Institute.

Blakemore, Ken, and Edwin Griggs. 2007. *Social Policy: An Introduction*. Third edition. Berkshire, England: McGraw-Hill.

Blumstein, Alfred. 1995. 'Youth violence, guns, and the illicit drug industry'. *Journal of Criminal Law and Criminology*, 86: 10–36.

Blumstein, Alfred. 2006. 'Disaggregating the violence trends'. In Alfred Blumstein and Joel Wallman (eds), *The Crime Drop in America*, revised edition. New York: Cambridge University Press.

Blumstein, Alfred, and Allen J. Beck. 2005. 'Re-entry as a transient state between liberty and recommitment'. In Jeremy Travis and Christy Visher (eds), *Prisoner Re-entry and Crime in America*. New York: Cambridge University Press.

Blumstein, Alfred, and Jacqueline Cohen. 1973. 'A theory of the stability of punishment'. *Journal of Criminal Law and Criminology*, 64: 198–207.

Blumstein, Alfred, Jacqueline Cohen, and Daniel Nagin. 1976. 'The dynamics of a homeostatic punishment process'. *Journal of Criminal Law and Criminology*, 67: 317–34.

Blumstein, Alfred, and Richard Rosenfeld. 1998. 'Explaining recent trends in US homicide rates'. *Journal of Criminal Law and Criminology*, 88: 1175–216.

Blumstein, Alfred, and Richard Rosenfeld. 2008. 'Factors contributing to US crime trends'. In Arthur S. Goldberger and Richard Rosenfeld (eds), *Understanding Crime Trends*. Washington, DC: National Academies Press.

Bohlen, Celestine. 1992. 'The Russians' new code: If it pays, anything goes'. *New York Times* (30 August).

Bourgois, Philippe. 1995. *In Search of Respect: Selling Crack in El Barrio*. New York: Cambridge University Press.

Boustan, Leah Platt. 2010. 'Was postwar suburbanization "white flight"? Evidence from the black migration'. *Quarterly Journal of Economics*, 125: 417–43.

Braga, Anthony A., and David L. Weisburd. 2010. *Policing Problem Places: Crime Hot Spots and Effective Prevention*. New York: Oxford University Press.

Braithwaite, John. 1981. 'The myth of social class and criminality reconsidered'. *American Sociological Review*, 46: 36–57.

Braithwaite, John. 1989. *Crime, Shame, and Reintegration*. Cambridge: Cambridge University Press.

Brantingham, Patricia L., and Paul J. Brantingham. 1993. 'Nodes, paths, and edges: Considerations on the complexity of crime and the physical environment'. *Environmental Psychology*, 13: 3–28.

Brennan, Morgan. 2011. 'Is the American Dream of home ownership dead? Not really'. *Forbes* (11 February).

Burgess, Robert, and Ronald L. Akers. 1966. 'A differential association-reinforcement theory of criminal behavior'. *Social Problems*, 14: 363–83.

Burke, Heather. 2008. 'Discount retailers see sales increase; consumers look for bargain to stretch dollar'. *USA Today* (9 May): 5A.

Bursik, Robert J. Jr. 1988. 'Social disorganization and theories of crime and delinquency: Problems and prospects'. *Criminology*, 26: 519–51.

Bursik, Robert J. Jr., and Harold Grasmick. 1993. *Neighborhoods and Crime: The Dimensions of Effective Community Control*. New York: Lexington.

Bushway, Shawn D. 2011. 'Labor markets and crime'. In James Q. Wilson and Joan Petersilia (eds), *Crime and Public Policy*. New York: Oxford University Press.

Bushway, Shawn, and Peter Reuter. 2011. 'Deterrence, economics, and the context of drug markets'. In Richard Rosenfeld, Kenna Quinet, and Crystal Garcia (eds), *Contemporary Issues in Criminological Theory and Research: The Role of Social Institutions*. Belmont, CA: Cengage.

Cantor, David, and Kenneth C. Land. 1985. 'Unemployment and crime rates in the Post-World War II United States: A theoretical and empirical analysis'. *American Sociological Review*, 50: 317–32.

Cavadino, Michael, and James Dignan. 2006. *Penal Systems: A Comparative Approach*. London: Sage.

Chainey, Spencer, and Jerry Ratcliffe. 2005. *GIS and Crime Mapping*. London: Wiley.

Chiricos, Theodore G. 1987. 'Rates of crime and unemployment: An analysis of aggregate research evidence'. *Social Problems*, 34: 187–212.

Clarke, Ronald V. (ed.) 1997. *Situational Crime Prevention: Successful Case Studies*. Second edition. Albany, NY: Harrow and Heston.

Cohen, Lawrence E., and Marcus Felson. 1979. 'Social change and crime rate trends: A routine activities approach'. *American Sociological Review*, 44: 588–608.

Cohen, Mark A. 2005. *The Costs of Crime and Justice*. New York: Routledge.

Cook, Philip J., and John H. Laub. 1998. 'The unprecedented epidemic in youth violence'. *Crime and Justice*, 24: 27–64.

Cook, Philip J., and John H. Laub. 2002. 'After the epidemic: Recent trends in youth violence in the United States'. *Crime and Justice*, 29: 1–37.

Cook, Philip J., and Gary A. Zarkin. 1985. 'Crime and the business cycle'. *Journal of Legal Studies*, 14: 115–28.

Cooney, Mark. 2009. *Is Killing Wrong?* Charlottesville, VA: University of Virginia Press.

Cork, Daniel. 1999. 'Examining space-time interaction in city-level homicide data: Crack markets and the diffusion of guns among youth'. *Journal of Quantitative Criminology*, 15: 379–406.

Cornish, Derek B., and Ronald V. Clarke (eds) 1986. *The Reasoning Criminal: Rational Choice Perspectives on Offending.* Secaucus, NJ: Springer.

Crandall, Russell. 2008. *Driven by Drugs: US Policy Toward Columbia.* Second edition. Boulder, CO: Lynne Rienner.

Crutchfield, Robert D. (forthcoming). *Work Matters: Jobs, Labor Markets and Crime.* New York: New York University Press.

Cullen, Francis T., and John Paul Wright. 1997. 'Liberating the anomie-strain paradigm: Implications from social-support theory'. In Nikos Passas and Robert Agnew (eds), *The Future of Anomie Theory.* Boston: Northeastern University Press.

Currie, Elliott. 1991. 'Crime in the market society' . *Dissent* (Spring): 251–9.

Currie, Elliott. 2012. 'Reaping what we sow: The impact of economic justice on criminal justice'. In Marc Mauer and Kate Epstein (eds), *To Build a Better Criminal Justice System: 25 Experts Envision the Next 25 Years of Reform.* Washington, DC: Sentencing Project.

DeFina, Robert H., and Thomas M. Arvanites. 2002. 'The weak effect of imprisonment on crime: 1971–1992'. *Social Science Quarterly,* 83: 635–53.

Devine, Joel A., Joseph F. Sheley, and M. Dwayne Smith. 1988. 'Macroeconomic and social-control policy influences on crime rate changes, 1948–1985'. *American Sociological Review,* 53: 407–20.

Diamond, Jared. 1992. *The Third Chimpanzee.* New York: HarperCollins.

Dolan, Chris J., John Freindreis, and Raymond Tatalovich. 2008. *The Presidency and Economic Policy.* Lanham, MD: Rowman & Littlefield.

Duffy, Brian, and Jeff Trimble. 1994. 'The wise guys of Russia'. *US News & World Report* (7 March).

Dunaway, R. Gregory, Francis T. Cullen, Velmer S. Burton Jr., and T. David Evans. 2000. 'The myth of social class and crime revisited: An examination of class and adult criminality'. *Criminology,* 38: 589–632.

Durkheim, Emile. 1964 [1893]. *The Division of Labor in Society.* New York: Free Press.

Durkheim, Emile. 1966 [1895]. *The Rules of the Sociological Method.* New York: Free Press.

Durlauf, Steven N., and Daniel S. Nagin. 2011. 'Imprisonment and crime: Can both be reduced?' *Criminology & Public Policy,* 10: 13–54.

Easterly, William and Stanley Fischer. 2001. 'Inflation and the poor'. *Journal of Money, Credit, and Banking,* 33: 160–78.

Eck, John, and David Weisburd. 1995. 'Crime places in crime theory'. In John E. Eck and David Weisburd (eds), *Crime and Place: Crime Prevention Studies.* Monsey, NY: Willow Tree Press.

Ehrlich, Isaac. 1973. 'Participation in illegitimate activities: A theoretical and empirical investigation'. *Journal of Political Economy,* 81: 521–65.

Eisner, Manuel. 2001. 'Modernization, self-control and lethal violence: The long-term dynamics of European homicide rates in theoretical perspective'. *British Journal of Criminology,* 41: 618–38.

Elliott, Delbert S., David Huizinga, and Suzanne S. Ageton. 1985. *Explaining Delinquency and Drug Use*. Newbury Park, CA: Sage.

Elliott, Dorinda. 1992. 'Russia's Goodfellas: The mafia on the Neva – How the mobs have taken over the markets'. *Newsweek* (12 October).

Erixon, Fredrik. 2011. 'Unease with modernity'. *New York Times* (28 July). http://www.nytimes.com/roomfordebate/2011/07/27/will-the-norway-massacre-deflate-europes-right-wing/unease-with-modernity. Accessed 27 March 2012.

Esping-Andersen, Gøsta. 1990. *The Three Worlds of Welfare Capitalism*. Princeton, NJ: Princeton University Press.

European Mortgage Federation. 2009. *HYPOSTAT 2008: A Review of Europe's Mortgage and Housing Markets*. Brussels, Belgium: EMF. http://www.hypo.org/Content/default.asp?pageId=578. Accessed 7 February 2012.

Fair, Ray C. 2009. 'Presidential and congressional vote-share equations'. *American Journal of Political Science* (January): 55–72.

Felson, Marcus. 2002. *Crime and Everyday Life*. Third edition. Thousand Oaks, CA: Sage.

Feuer, Lewis S. (ed.) 1959. *Marx & Engels: Basic Writings on Politics & Philosophy*. Garden City, NY: Anchor Books.

Field, Simon. 1990. *Trends in Crime and Their Interpretation: A Study of Recorded Crime in Post War England and Wales*. London: Her Majesty's Stationery Office.

Figes, Orlando. 1996. *A People's Tragedy: The Russian Revolution, 1891–1924*. London: Jonathan Cape.

Fishbein, Diana. 2001. *Biobehavioral Perspectives in Criminology*. Belmont, CA: Wadsworth.

Fourcade, Marion, and Kieran Healy. 2007. 'Moral views of market society'. *Annual Review of Sociology*, 33: 285–311.

Freeman, Richard B. 1996. 'Why do so many young American men commit crimes and what might we do about it?' *Journal of Economic Perspectives*, 10: 25–42.

Garland, David. 1990. *Punishment and Modern Society: A Study in Social Theory*. Chicago: University of Chicago Press.

Garland, David. 2001. *The Culture of Control: Crime and Social Order in Contemporary Society*. Chicago: University of Chicago Press.

Garland, David. 2010. *Peculiar Institution: America's Death Penalty in an Age of Abolition*. Cambridge, MA: Harvard University Press.

Gartner, Rosemary. 1991. 'Family structure, welfare spending, and child homicide in developed democracies'. *Journal of Marriage and the Family*, 53: 231–40.

Gerth, Hans, and C. Wright Mills. 1964. *Character and Social Structure: The Psychology of Social Institutions*. New York: Harcourt.

Gibson, Campbell, and Kay Jung. 2005. *Historical Census Statistics on Population Totals by Race, 1790 to 1990, and by Hispanic Origin, 1970 to 1990, for Large Cities and Other Urban Places in the United States by Population Division*. Working paper No. 76. Washington, DC: US Census Bureau (http://www.

census.gov/population/www/documentation/twps0076/twps0076.html). Accessed 24 May 2011.

Gobert, James, and Maurice Punch. 2000. '*Whistle-*blowing and the Public Interest Disclosure Act 1998'. *Modern Law Review*, 63: 25–54.

Golub, Andrew Lang and Bruce D. Johnson. 1997. 'Crack's decline: Some surprises across US cities'. *National Institute of Justice: Research in Brief.* Washington, DC: US Department of Justice.

Goode, Erich (ed.) 2008. *Out of Control: Assessing the General Theory of Crime.* Stanford, CA: Stanford University Press.

Gottfredson, Michael, and Travis Hirschi. 1990. *A General Theory of Crime.* Stanford, CA: Stanford University Press.

Gottschalk, Marie. 2006. *The Prison and the Gallows: The Politics of Mass Incarceration in America.* New York: Cambridge University Press.

Gould, Eric D., Bruce A. Weinberg, and David B. Mustard. 2002. 'Crime rates and local labor market opportunities in the United States: 1979–1997'. *Review of Economics and Statistics*, 84: 45–61.

Granovetter, Mark. 1985. 'Economic action and social structure: The problem of embeddedness'. *American Journal of Sociology*, 91: 481–510.

Greenwood, Peter W., Karyn Model, C. Peter Rydell, and James Chiesa. 1998. *Diverting Children from a Life of Crime.* Santa Monica, CA: RAND Corporation.

Grogger, Jeffrey T. 1998. 'Market wages and youth crime'. *Journal of Labor Economics*, 16: 756–91.

Guerino, Paul, Paige M. Harrison, and William J. Sabol. 2011. *Prisoners in 2010.* Washington, DC: US Department of Justice. http://bjs.ojp.usdoj.gov/content/pub/pdf/p10.pdf. Accessed 20 March 2012.

Heimer, Karen. 1990. 'Socioeconomic status, subcultural definitions, and violent delinquency'. *Social Forces*, 75: 799–833.

Hempel, Carl. 1966. *Philosophy of Natural Science.* Englewood Cliffs, NJ: Prentice-Hall.

Hindelang, Michael, Michael Gottfredson, and James Garofalo. 1978. *Victims of Personal Crime: An Empirical Foundation for a Theory of Personal Victimization.* Cambridge, MA: Ballinger.

Hirschi, Travis. 1969. *Causes of Delinquency.* Berkeley, CA: University of California Press.

Hirschman, Albert O. 1992. *Rival Views of Market Society and Other Recent Essays.* Cambridge, MA: Harvard University Press.

Huang, Youqin, and Setha M. Low. 2008. 'Is gating always exclusionary? A comparative analysis of gated communities in American and Chinese cities'. In John R. Logan (eds), *Urban China in Transition.* Malden, MA: Blackwell.

Hughes, Kristen A. 2006. *Justice Expenditure and Employment in the United States, 2003.* Washington, DC: US Department of Justice.

Jackall, Robert. 1988. *Dirty Business: Exploring Corporate Misconduct and Moral Mazes.* New York: Oxford University Press.

Jackson, Anna-Louise, and Anthony Feld. 2011. 'Accelerating inflation spurs consumer "trade down" to McDonald's, Wal-Mart'. *Bloomberg News* (16 June). http://www.bloomberg.com/news/2011-06-17/faster-inflation-causes-trade-down-to-mcdonald-s-wal-mart.html. Accessed 18 February 2012.

Jacobs, Bruce A. 1999. *Dealing Crack: The Social World of Streetcorner Selling.* Boston: Northeastern University Press.

Jacobs, Bruce A. 2000. *Robbing Drug Dealers.* New Brunswick, NJ: Aldine.

Jacobs, Bruce A., and Richard Wright. 2006. *Street Justice: Retaliation in the Criminal Underworld.* New York: Cambridge University Press.

James, Doris J. 2004. *Profile of Jail Inmates, 2002.* Washington, DC: US Department of Justice.

Johnson, Ryan S., Shawn Kantor, and Price V. Fishback. 2007. 'Striking at the roots of crime: The impact of social welfare spending on crime during the Great Depression'. *National Bureau of Economic Research.* Working paper no. 12825 (January).

Kahneman, Daniel. 2011. *Thinking, Fast and Slow.* New York: Farrar, Straus and Giroux.

Karstedt, Susanne. 2003. 'Legacies of a culture of inequality: The Janus-Face of crime in post-communist societies'. *Crime, Law and Social Change,* 40: 295–320.

Karstedt, Susanne. 2010. 'The new institutionalism in criminology: Approaches, theories, and themes'. In Eugene McLaughlin and Tim Newburn (eds), *The Sage Handbook of Criminological Theory.* London: Sage.

Kenney, Dennis J., and James O. Finckenauer. 1995. *Organized Crime in America.* Belmont, CA: Wadsworth.

Kornhauser, Ruth R. 1978. *Social Sources of Delinquency: An Appraisal of Analytic Models.* Chicago: University of Chicago Press.

Kubrin, Charis E., and Ronald Weitzer. 2003. 'New directions in social disorganization theory'. *Journal of Research in Crime and Delinquency,* 40: 374–402.

Kyckelhahn, Tracey. 2011. *Justice Expenditures and Employment, FY 1982–2007 – Statistical Tables.* Washington, DC: US Department of Justice. http://bjs.ojp.usdoj.gov/content/pub/pdf/jee8207st.pdf. Accessed 22 March 2012.

Lacey, Nicola. 2008. *The Prisoners' Dilemma: Political Economy and Punishment in Contemporary Democracies.* Cambridge, UK: Cambridge University Press.

LaFree, Gary. 1998. *Losing Legitimacy: Street Crime and the Decline of Social Institutions in America.* Boulder, CO: Westview.

Lahey, Benjamin B., Terrie E. Moffitt, and Avshalom Caspi (eds) 2003. *Causes of Conduct Disorder and Juvenile Delinquency.* New York: Guilford Press.

Lauritsen, Janet L., and Karen Heimer. 2010. 'Violent victimization among males and economic conditions'. *Criminology & Public Policy,* 9: 665–92.

Lemann, Nicholas. 1991. *The Promised Land: The Great Black Migration and How It Changed America*. New York: Knopf.

Levitt, Steven F. 1996. 'The effect of prison population size on crime rates: Evidence from prison overcrowding litigation'. *Quarterly Journal of Economics*, 111: 319–51.

Liedka, Raymond V., Anne Morrison Piehl, and Bert Useem. 2006. 'The crime-control effect of incarceration: Does scale matter?' *Criminology & Public Policy*, 5: 245–76.

Loeber, Rolf, and David P. Farrington (eds) 1998. *Serious and Violent Juvenile Offenders: Risk Factors and Successful Interventions*. Thousand Oaks, CA: Sage.

Loeber, Rolf, and David P. Farrington. 2011. *Young Homicide Offenders and Victims: Risk Factors, Prediction, and Prevention from Childhood*. New York: Springer.

Loeber, Rolf, and Magda Stouthamer-Loeber. 1998. 'Development of juvenile aggression and violence: Some common misconceptions and controversies'. *American Psychologist*, 53: 242–59.

Mankiw, N. Gregory. 2009. *Principles of Economics*. Fifth edition. Mason, OH: Cengage.

Manza, Jeff and Christopher Uggen. 2006. *Locked Out: Felon Disenfranchisement and American Democracy*. New York: Oxford University Press.

Marx, Gary T. 1985. 'The surveillance society: The threat of 1984-style techniques'. *The Futurist* (June): 21–6.

Marx, Karl, and Friedrich Engels. 1969 [1852]. *Selected Works*. Volume one. Moscow: Progress Publishers.

Massey, Douglas, and Nancy Denton. 1993. *American Apartheid: Segregation and the Making of the Underclass*. Cambridge, MA: Harvard University Press.

Matza, David, and Gresham Sykes. 1961. 'Juvenile delinquency and subterranean values'. *American Sociological Review*, 26: 712–19.

Merton, Robert K. 1936. 'The unanticipated consequences of purposive social action'. *American Sociological Review*, 1: 894–904.

Merton, Robert K. 1938.' Social structure and anomie'. *American Sociological Review*, 3: 672–82.

Merton, Robert K. 1968. *Social Theory and Social Structure*. New York: Free Press.

Merton, Robert K. 1976. *Sociological Ambivalence and Other Essays*. New York: Free Press.

Messner, Steven F. 2012. 'Morality, markets, and the ASC: 2011 Presidential Address to the American Society of Criminology'. *Criminology*, 50: 5–25.

Messner, Steven F., Luc Anselin, Robert D. Baller, Darnell F. Hawkins, Glenn Deane, and Stewart E. Tolnay. 1999. 'The spatial patterning of county homicide rates: An application of exploratory spatial data analysis'. *Journal of Quantitative Criminology*, 15: 423–50.

Messner, Steven F., Glenn D. Deane, Luc Anselin, and Benjamin Pearson-Nelson. 2005. 'Locating the vanguard in rising and falling homicide rates across US cities'. *Criminology*, 43: 661–96.

Messner, Steven F., Lawrence E. Raffalovich, and Peter Shrock. 2002. 'Reassessing the cross-national relationship between income inequality and homicide rates: The implications of data quality control in the measurement of income distribution'. *Journal of Quantitative Criminology*, 18: 377–95.

Messner, Steven F., Lawrence E. Raffalovich, and Gretchen M. Sutton. 2010. 'Poverty, infant mortality, and homicide rates in cross-national perspective: Assessments of criterion and construct validity'. *Criminology*, 48: 509–37.

Messner, Steven F., and Richard Rosenfeld. 1997. 'Political restraint of the market and levels of criminal homicide: A cross-national application of institutional-anomie theory'. *Social Forces*, 75: 1393–416.

Messner, Steven F., and Richard Rosenfeld. 2000. 'Market dominance, crime, and globalisation'. In Susanne Karstedt and Kai D. Bussmann (eds), *Social Dynamics of Crime and Control: New Theories for a World in Transition*. Portland, OR: Hart Publishing, pp. 13–26.

Messner, Steven F., and Richard Rosenfeld. 2007a. *Crime and the American Dream*. Fourth edition. Belmont, CA: Wadsworth.

Messner, Steven F., and Richard Rosenfeld. 2007b. '"Institutionalizing" criminological theory'. In Joan McCord (ed.), *Institutions and Intentions in the Study of Crime: Beyond Empiricism*, Volume 13 of *Advances in Criminological Theory*. New Brunswick, NJ: Transaction.

Messner, Steven F., Richard Rosenfeld, and Susanne Karstedt. 2011. 'Social institutions and crime'. In Francis T. Cullen and Pamela Wilcox (eds), *Oxford Handbook of Criminological Theory*. New York: Oxford University Press.

Messner, Steven F., Raymond H. C. Teske, Jr., Robert D. Baller, and Helmut Thome. 2012. 'Structural covariates of violent crime rates in Germany: Exploratory spatial analyses of Kreise.' *Justice Quarterly* (forthcoming).

Milgram, Stanley. 1974. *Obedience to Authority*. New York: Harper & Row.

Miller, Walter. 1958. 'Lower-class culture as a generating milieu of gang delinquency'. *Journal of Social Issues*, 14: 5–19.

Mills, C. Wright. 1943. 'The professional ideology of social pathologists'. *American Journal of Sociology*, 49: 165–80.

Mills, C. Wright. 1959. *The Sociological Imagination*. New York: Oxford University Press.

Miron, Jeffrey A. 1999. 'Violence and the US prohibitions of drugs and alcohol'. *American Law and Economics Review*, 1–2: 78–114.

Miron, Jeffrey A., and Jeffrey Zwiebel. 1991. 'Alcohol consumption during Prohibition'. *American Economic Review*, 81: 242–7.

Moffitt, Terrie E. 2005. 'The new look of behavioral genetics in developmental psychopathology: Gene–environment interplay in antisocial behaviors'. *Psychological Bulletin*, 131: 533–54.

Morenoff, Jeffrey D., Robert J. Sampson, and Stephen W. Raudenbush. 2001. 'Neighborhood inequality, collective efficacy, and the spatial dynamics of urban violence'. *Criminology*, 39: 517–59.

Murray, Charles. 1984. *Losing Ground: American Social Policy, 1950–1980*. New York: Basic Books.

Nagin, Daniel S. 1998. 'Criminal deterrence research at the outset of the twenty-first century'. In Michael Tonry (ed.), *Crime and Justice: An Annual Review of Research*, Volume 23. Chicago: University of Chicago Press.

New York Times. 1929. '7 Chicago gangsters slain by firing squad of rivals, some in police uniforms'. http://www.nytimes.com/learning/general/onthisday/big/0214.html#article. Accessed 23 February 2012.

New York Times. 2012a. 'Mexican drug trafficking (Mexico's drug war)'. http://topics.nytimes.com/top/news/international/countriesandterritories/mexico/drug_trafficking/index.html. Accessed 25 February 2012.

New York Times. 2012b. 'Foreclosures (2012 Robosigning and foreclosure abuse settlement)'. http://topics.nytimes.com/top/reference/timestopics/subjects/f/foreclosures/index.html. Accessed 25 February 2012.

Nguyen, Tomson H., and Henry N. Pontell. 2010. 'Mortgage origination fraud and the global economic crisis: A criminological analysis'. *Criminology & Public Policy*, 9: 591–612.

North, Douglas C. 1990. *Institutions, Institutional Change and Economic Performance*. Cambridge, UK: Cambridge University Press.

Orru, Marco. 1987. *Anomie: History and Meanings*. Boston: Allen & Unwin.

Ousey, Graham, and Matthew R. Lee. 2002. 'Examining the Conditional Nature of the Illicit Drug Market-Homicide Relationship: A Partial Test of the Theory of Contingent Causation'. *Criminology*, 40: 73–102.

Owens, Emily Greene. 2011. 'The birth of organized crime? The American temperance movement and market-based violence'. Available at SSRN: http://dx.doi.org/10.2139/ssrn.1865347. Accessed 23 February 2012.

Pager, Devah. 2007. *Marked: Race, Crime, and Finding Work in an Era of Mass Incarceration*. Chicago: University of Chicago Press.

Pampel, Fred N., and Rosemary Gartner. 1995. 'Age structure, socio-political institutions, and national homicide rates'. *European Sociological Review*, 11: 243–60.

Parenti, Christian. 2003. *The Soft Cage: Surveillance in America from Slavery to the War on Terror*. New York: Basic Books.

Parsons, Talcott. 1951. *The Social System*. New York: Free Press.

Parsons, Talcott. 1990 [1934]. 'Prolegomena to a theory of social institutions'. *American Sociological Review*, 55: 319–33.

Pattillo, Mary, David F. Weiman, and Bruce Western (eds) 2004. *Imprisoning America: The Social Effects of Mass Incarceration*. New York: Russell Sage Foundation.

Peart, Nicholas L. 2011. 'Why is the N.Y.P.D. after me?' *New York Times* (17 December). http://www.nytimes.com/2011/12/18/opinion/sunday/young-black-and-frisked-by-the-nypd.html?pagewanted=all. Accessed 23 March 2012.

Petersilia, Joan. 2003. *When Prisoners Come Home: Parole and Prisoner Re-entry*. New York: Oxford University Press.

Polanyi, Karl. 1957 [1944]. *The Great Transformation: The Political and Economic Origins of Our Time*. Boston: Beacon Press.

Pontell, Henry N., and William K. Black. 2012. 'White-collar criminology and the occupy Wall Street movement'. *Criminologist*, 37: 1, 3–6.

Prasad, Monica. 2006. *The Politics of Free Markets: The Rise of Neoliberal Economic Policies in Britain, France, Germany, and the United States*. Chicago: University of Chicago Press.

Pratt, Travis C., and Francis T. Cullen. 2000. 'The empirical status of Gottfredson and Hirschi's general theory of crime: A meta-analysis'. *Criminology*, 38: 931–64.

Pratt, Travis C., and Francis T. Cullen. 2005. 'Assessing macro-level predictors and theories of crime: A meta-analysis'. In Michael Tonry (ed.), *Crime and Justice: A Review of Research*. Volume 32. Chicago: University of Chicago Press.

Pridemore, William A., Mitchell B. Chamlin, and John K. Cochran. 2007. 'An interrupted time series analysis of Durkheim's social deregulation thesis: The case of the Russian Federation'. *Justice Quarterly*, 24: 271–90.

Pridemore, William A., and Sang-Weon Kim. 2006. 'Democratization and political change as threats to collective sentiments: Testing Durkheim in Russia'. *Annals of the American Academy of Political and Social Science*, 605: 82–103.

Rafter, Nicole. 1997. *Creating Born Criminals*. Champaign, IL: University of Illinois Press.

Rafter, Nicole. 2008. *The Criminal Brain: Understanding Biological Theories of Crime*. New York: New York University Press.

Rainwater, Lee. 1970. 'The problem of lower class culture'. *Journal of Social Issues*, 26: 133–48.

Ralston, Roy W. 1999. 'Economy and race: Interactive determinants of property crime in the United States, 1958–1995'. *American Journal of Economics and Sociology*, 58: 405–34.

Raphael, Steven, and Rudolf Winter-Ebmer. 2001. 'Identifying the effect of unemployment on crime'. *Journal of Law and Economics*, 44: 259–83.

Rebellon, Cesar J., Nicole Leeper Piquero, Alex R. Piquero, and Sherod Thaxton. 2009. 'Do frustrated economic expectations and objective economic inequity promote crime? A randomized experiment testing Agnew's general strain theory'. *European Journal of Criminology*, 6: 47–71.

Reiman, Jeffrey, and Paul Leighton. 2009. *The Rich Get Richer and the Poor Get Prison: Ideology, Class, and Criminal Justice*. Ninth edition. Upper Saddle River, NJ: Prentice Hall.

Reuter, Peter (ed.) 2010. *Understanding the Demand for Illegal Drugs*. Washington, DC: National Academies Press.

Rodman, Hyman. 1963. 'The lower-class value stretch'. *Social Forces*, 42: 205–15.

Rosenbloom, Stephanie. 2008. 'Thrift shops thriving, but running low on stock'. *New York Times* (10 September): C1, C8.

Rosenfeld, Richard. 2009. 'Crime is the problem: Homicide, acquisitive crime, and economic conditions'. *Journal of Quantitative Criminology*, 25: 287–306.

Rosenfeld, Richard. 2011a. 'Changing crime rates'. In James Q. Wilson and Joan Petersilia (eds), *Crime and Public Policy*. New York: Oxford University Press.

Rosenfeld, Richard. 2011b. 'The big picture: 2010 presidential address to the American Society of Criminology'. *Criminology*, 49: 1–26.

Rosenfeld, Richard, Timothy M. Bray, and Arlen Egley. 1999. 'Facilitating violence: A comparison of gang-motivated, gang-affiliated, and non-gang youth homicides'. *Journal of Quantitative Criminology*, 15: 495–516.

Rosenfeld, Richard, and Robert Fornango. 2007. The impact of economic conditions on robbery and property crime: The role of consumer sentiment. *Criminology*, 45: 735–69.

Rosenfeld, Richard, and Steven F. Messner. 2006. 'The origins, nature, and prospects of institutional-anomie theory'. In Stuart Henry and Mark Lanier (eds), *The Essential Criminology Reader*. Boulder, CO: Westview.

Rosenfeld, Richard, and Steven F. Messner. 2007. 'Economic cycles, the welfare state, and homicide, 1971–2001'. Paper presented at the meeting of the American Society of Criminology, Atlanta, GA (November).

Rosenfeld, Richard, and Steven F. Messner. 2009. 'The crime drop in comparative perspective: The impact of the economy and imprisonment on American and European burglary rates'. *British Journal of Sociology*, 60: 445–71.

Rosenfeld, Richard, and Steven F. Messner. 2010. ' The normal crime rate, the economy, and mass incarceration: An institutional-anomie perspective on crime-control policy'. In Scott Decker and Hugh Barlow (eds), *Criminology and Public Policy: Putting Theory to Work*. Philadelphia: Temple University Press.

Roth, Randolph. 2009. *American Homicide*. Cambridge, MA: Harvard University Press.

Rothstein, Bo. 1998. *Just Institutions Matter: The Moral and Political Logic of the Universal Welfare State*. Cambridge, UK: Cambridge University Press.

Rusche, George, and Otto Kirchheimer. 2003 [1939]. *Punishment and Social Structure*. Piscataway, NJ: Transaction.

Sampson, Robert J. 2002. 'Transcending tradition: New directions in community research, Chicago style'. *Criminology*, 40: 213–30.

Sampson, Robert J. 2006. 'Collective efficacy theory: Lessons learned and directions for future inquiry'. In Francis T. Cullen, John Paul Wright, and Kristie R. Blevins (eds), *Taking Stock: The Status of Criminological Theory*. Advances in Criminological Theory, Volume 15. New Brunswick, NJ: Transaction.

Sampson, Robert J., and Lydia Bean. 2006. 'Cultural mechanisms and killing fields: A revised theory of community-level racial inequality'. In Ruth D. Peterson, Lauren J. Krivo, and John Hagan (eds), *The Many Colors of Crime: Inequalities of Race, Ethnicity, and Crime in America*. New York: New York University Press.

Sampson, Robert J., and W. Byron Groves. 1989. 'Community structure and crime: Testing social-disorganization theory'. *American Journal of Sociology*, 94: 774–802.

Sampson, Robert J., and John H. Laub. 1993. *Crime in the Making: Pathways and Turning Points Through Life*. Cambridge, MA: Harvard University Press.

Sampson, Robert J., and Janet L. Lauritsen. 1990. 'Deviant lifestyles, proximity to crime, and the offender-victim link in personal violence'. *Journal of Research in Crime and Delinquency*, 27: 110–39.

Sampson, Robert J., Jeffrey D. Morenoff, and T. Gannon-Rowley. 2002. 'Assessing "neighborhood effects": Social processes and new directions in research'. *Annual Review of Sociology*, 28: 443–78.

Sampson, Robert J., Stephen W. Raudenbush, and Felton Earls. 1997. 'Neighborhoods and violent crime: A multilevel study of collective efficacy'. *Science*, 277: 918–24.

Savage, Joanne, Richard R. Bennett, and Mona Danner. 2008. 'Economic assistance and crime: A cross-national investigation'. *European Journal of Criminology*, 5: 217–38.

Savolainen, Jukka. 2000. 'Inequality, welfare state, and homicide: Further support for the institutional anomie theory'. *Criminology*, 38: 1021–42.

Schwartz, Barry. 1994. *The Costs of Living*. New York: Norton.

Schwartz, Barry. 2012. 'Economics made easy: Think friction'. *New York Times Sunday Review* (19 February): 5, 9.

Scruggs, Lyle. 2004. 'Welfare state entitlements data set: A comparative institutional analysis of eighteen Welfare States, Version 1.1'. http://sp.uconn.edu/~scruggs/wp.htm. Accessed 12 July 2012.

Shaw, Clifford R., and Henry D. McKay. 1969. *Juvenile Delinquency in Urban Areas*. Revised edition. Chicago: University of Chicago Press.

Sheley, Joseph F., and James D. Wright. 1995. *In the Line of Fire: Youth, Guns, and Violence in Urban America.* Hawthorne, NY: Aldine.

Shelley, Louise I. 1981. *Crime and Modernization: The Impact of Industrialization and Urbanization on Crime.* Carbondale, IL: Southern Illinois University Press.

Sherman, Matthew. 2009. *A Short History of Financial Deregulation in the United States.* Washington, DC: Center for Economic and Policy Research.

Simkovic, Michael. 2009. 'Secret liens and the financial crisis of 2008'. *American Bankruptcy Law Journal,* 83: 253–96.

Simon, Jonathan. 1993. *Poor Discipline: Parole and the Social Control of the Underclass, 1890–1990.* Chicago: University of Chicago Press.

Skocpol, Theda, and Vanessa Williamson. 2012. *The Tea Party and the Remaking of Republican Conservatism.* New York: Oxford University Press.

Smelser, Neil J., and Richard Swedberg. 1994. 'The sociological perspective on the economy'. In N.J. Smelser and R. Swedberg (eds), *The Handbook of Economic Sociology.* Princeton, NJ: Princeton University Press.

Spelman, William. 2006. 'The limited importance of prison expansion'. In Alfred Blumstein and Joel Wallman (eds), *The Crime Drop in America.* Revised edition. New York: Cambridge University Press.

Stanley, Alessandra. 1994. 'Sexual harassment thrives in the new Russian climate'. *New York Times* (17 April).

Stark, Rodney. 1987. 'Deviant places: A theory of the ecology of crime'. *Criminology,* 25: 893–909.

Stewart, Eric A., Christopher J. Schreck, and Ronald L. Simons. 2006. '"I ain't gonna let no one disrespect me": Does the code of the street reduce or increase violent victimization among African American adolescents?' *Journal of Research in Crime and Delinquency,* 43: 427–58.

Sullivan, Mercer L. 1989. *Getting Paid: Youth Crime and Work in the Inner City.* Ithaca, NY: Cornell University Press.

Sutherland, Edwin H. 1986. *White Collar Crime: The Uncut Version.* New Haven, CT: Yale University Press.

Sutton, Mike. 1995. 'Supply by theft: Does the market for second-hand goods play a role in keeping crime figures high?' *British Journal of Criminology,* 38: 400–16.

Sutton, Mike. 1998. 'Handling stolen goods and theft: A market reduction approach'. *Home Office Research Study 178.* London: Home Office.

Sutton, Willie and Linn, Edward. 2004. *Where the money was: The memoirs of a Bank Robber.* New York: Broadway Books.

Tang, Chor Foon, and Hooi Hooi Lean. 2007. 'Will inflation increase crime rate? New evidence from bounds and modified Wald tests'. *Global Crime,* 8: 311–23.

Temin, Peter. 2010. 'The Great Recession and the Great Depression'. *National Bureau of Economic Research.* Working paper no. 15645 (January).

Tittle, Charles R., Wayne J. Villemez, and Douglas A. Smith. 1978. 'The myth of social class and criminality: An empirical assessment of the empirical evidence'. *American Sociological Review*, 43: 643–56.

Tonry, Michael. 1996. *Malign Neglect: Race, Crime, and Punishment in America*. New York: Oxford University Press.

Tonry, Michael. 2004. *Thinking About Crime: Sense and Sensibility in American Penal Culture*. New York: Oxford University Press.

Travis, Jeremy, and Christy Visher (eds) 2005. *Prisoner Re-entry and Crime in America*. New York: Cambridge University Press.

Truman, Jennifer L., and Michael R. Rand. 2010. *Criminal Victimization, 2009*. Washington, DC: US Department of Justice.

Turner, Jonathon H. 2003. *Human Institutions: A Theory of Societal Evolution*. Lanham, MD: Rowman & Littlefield.

Uchitelle, Louis. 2010. 'Volcker pushes for reform, regretting past silence'. *New York Times* (10 July). http://www.nytimes.com/2010/07/11/business/11volcker.html?pagewanted=all. Accessed 28 February 2012.

Venkatesh, Sudhir Alladi. 2006. *Off the Books: The Underground Economy of the Urban Poor*. Cambridge, MA: Harvard University Press.

Vold, George B. 1958. *Theoretical Criminology*. New York: Oxford.

Weber, Max. 1976 [1904–05]. *The Protestant Ethic and the Spirit of Capitalism*. With an introduction by Anthony Giddens. New York: Scribner's.

Weisburd, David, and Gerben Bruinsma. 2009. 'Units of analysis in geographic criminology: Historical development, critical issues and open questions'. In David Weisburd and Gerben Bruinsma (eds), *Putting Crime in Its Place: Units of Analysis in Spatial Crime Research*. New York: Springer Verlaag.

Welsh, Brandon, and Alex Piquero. 2011. 'Investing where it counts: Preventing delinquency and crime with early family-based programs'. In Richard Rosenfeld, Kenna Quinet, and Crystal Garcia (eds), *Contemporary Issues in Criminological Theory and Research: The Role of Social Institutions*. Belmont, CA: Cengage.

Western, Bruce. 2006. *Punishment and Inequality in America*. New York: Russell Sage Foundation.

Wikström, Per-Olof H. 2006. 'Individuals, settings and acts of crime: Situational mechanisms and the explanation of crime'. In P.-O. H. Wikström and R.J. Sampson (eds), *The Explanation of Crime: Context, Mechanisms and Development*. Cambridge: Cambridge University Press.

Wikström, Per-Olof H. 2010. 'Explaining crime as moral action'. In S. Hitlin and S. Vaysey (eds), *Handbook of the Sociology of Morality*. New York: Springer.

Wikström, Per-Olof H. 2011. 'Does everything matter? Addressing the problem of causation and explanation in the study of crime'. In Jean M. McGloin, Christopher J. Silverman, and Leslie W. Kennedy (eds), *When Crime Appears: The Role of Emergence*. New York: Routledge.

Wilkinson, Richard G., and Kate Pickett. 2009. *The Spirit Level: Why More Equal Societies Almost Always Do Better*. New York: Allen Lane.

Wilson, James Q. 1985. *Thinking About Crime*. Revised edition. New York: Vintage.

Wilson, William Julius. 1980. *The Declining Significance of Race: Blacks and Changing American Institutions*. Second edition. Chicago: University of Chicago Press.

Wilson, William Julius. 1987. *The Truly Disadvantaged: The Inner City, the Underclass, and Public Policy*. Chicago: University of Chicago Press.

Wolfe, Alan. 1989. *Whose Keeper? Social Science and Moral Obligation*. Berkeley, CA: University of California Press.

Wolfgang, Marvin E., and Franco Ferracuti. 1967. *The Subculture of Violence: Towards an Integrated Theory in Criminology*. London: Tavistock.

Wright, Richard T., and Scott H. Decker. 1994. *Burglars On The Job: Streetlife and Residential Break-Ins*. Boston: Northeastern University Press.

Wright, Richard T., and Scott H. Decker. 1997. *Armed Robbers in Action: Stickups and Street Culture*. Boston: Northeastern University Press.

Wrong, Dennis H. 1961. 'The oversocialized conception of man in modern sociology'. *American Sociological Review*, 26: 183–93.

index

Page numbers in *italics* refer to figures and tables.

acquisitive crime *see* property/
acquisitive crime
Adler, W.M. 91
African-Americans *see* ethnicity
Agnew, R. 28–9
Akers, R.L. 27–8, 33
Allen, R.C. 81
Anderson, E. 37, 45–7, 49, 114
anomie
'anomic division of
labour' 75
ethic of 64–6
institutional-anomie theory
(IAT) 60–2, 69–70,
71–3, 76
attachment
community 42–3
family/parental 34, 35

balance of power, institutional
61, 117
banking regulation and
deregulation 95–6
biological theories 26–7
biosocial theories 27, 33
Black, W.K. 94, 95
Blumstein, A. 90, 93
and Beck, A.J. 104
and Cohen, J. 100

Blumstein, A. *cont.*
et al. 100
and Rosenfeld, R. 90
Bohlen, C. 74
Braithewaite, J. 36
burglary *5*, 16–17
see also routine activities
Bursik, R.J. Jr. and Grasmick,
H. 37, 44
Bushway, S. 79
and Reuter, P. 111, 112

capitalist societies *see* market
capitalism
causal processes 7–9
causes
of causes 31, 34–5
and manifestations 48
proximate 106–9
Chicago and Chicago
School 40–3, 44–5, 47,
49–51, 89
cocaine/crack 90–1, 92–3
code of the street (subculture)
43, 45–7, 48–9
Cohen, L.E. and Felson, M.
37, 38
collective efficacy 44–5
commitment 34

community-level analysis
    36–48
    and economic conditions
        48–52
    and individual-level analysis
        42–3
conditional effects 8, 9, 14–15
consumer sentiment 79–80
control(s)
    motivations and
        opportunities 20–1, 23,
        31–6, 102, 106–9
    self-control 25–6, 30–1, 35
    see also social control
Cornish, D.B. and Clarke, R.V.
    25
costs of mass incarceration
    103–6
counter-norms 58
crack/cocaine 90–1, 92–3
cross-national comparisons
    household income and
        burglary victimization
        16–17
    social welfare provisions
        14–15, 72–3
cultural deviance theory
    46–7
Currie, E. 101

decision-making see rational
    choice theory
demand
    and control in underground
        markets 83–6
    economic rhythms and
        77–86
    regulation of 87–97
    supply and 111–14
Devine, J.A. et al. 83
disadvantage see
    socioeconomic status

disorganized communities and
    social control 40–5
drug markets 90–3
Duffy, B. and Trimble, J. 74
Durkheim, E. 56, 57, 60, 75,
    76–7, 100

economic conditions
    community-level analysis
        48–52
    individual-level analysis
        31–6
economic dominance 53–4,
    61–6, 69, 70, 73
economic rhythms 77–86,
    107–9
Ehrlich, I. 22–3, 83, 84
Elliot, D. 73
emotions 28–9, 33–4
Esping-Anderson, G. 71
ethics
    anomic 64–6
    Protestant 65
ethnicity
    Chicago 40–1, 42, 49–51
    homicides and illicit drug
        markets 90
    prisoners 104

family/parental attachment
    34, 35
financial crisis (2008) 80–1,
    95–7, 118
firearms violence 90

gang homicides 5–7
GDP: cross-national
    comparison 16–17
general strain theory
    28–9, 33–4
Gottfredson, M. and Hirschi, T.
    25–6, 35

Granovetter, M. 63, 64
Great Depression 80–1, 95,
    100, 118
guardianship 38–9

Hempel, C. 19, 98
Hirschi, T. 29, 34, 43, 63
homicides
  and acquisitive crime 10–12
  and illicit drug markets 90
  and institutional
      deregulation, Russia
      76–7
  and Prohibition 89
  proximate causes 106
  and socioeconomic status
      5–7
  and welfare system
    Russia 72–3
    unemployment 14–15, 72
household income
  and burglary victimization
      16–17
  and theft victimization
      12–13
housing crisis 93–5

illegal markets
  and level of analysis 109–15
  stolen goods 83–6
illicit alcohol and drugs 88–93
illicit commodities 87–9
'incapacitation effect' of
    incarceration 102
individual-level analysis 21–31
  and community-level
      analysis 42–3
  and economic conditions
      31–6
inflation 81–3, 85–6
institutional-anomie theory
    (IAT) 60–2, 69–70, 71–3, 76

institutions 54–7
  analysis 57–60, 68–9
  balance of power 61, 117
  economic dominance 53–4,
      61–6, 69, 70, 73
  interdependence 60–1
  performance 59–60, 62–3,
      77–86, 108–9
  regulation 58–9, 63–6, 73–7,
      108–9, 115–19
  structure 58, 60, 61, 62, 70–3

Karstedt, S. 54, 57
Kennedy, D.J. and
    Finckenaurer, J.O. 92–3

labour market
  legitimate 91–2
  and prison population
      100–1
  see also unemployment
LaFree, G. 83, 118
level of analysis 8, 9, 16–17
  and illegal markets 109–15
  see also community-level
      analysis; individual-level
      analysis
Loeber, R. and Stouthamer-
    Loeber, M. 110
Lombroso, C. 26–7

market capitalism
  economic dominance 53–4,
      61–6, 69, 70, 73
  economic rhythms 77–86,
      107–9
  post-Soviet Russia 73–7
  regulation and crime control
      115–19
  taming 70–3
Marx, K. 98
  and Engels, F. 24

mediated effects 8, *9*, 10–13, 18
Merton, R.K. 64, 88, 91–2, 96, 108
Messner, S.F.
 et al. 75
 see also Rosenfeld, R.
Miller, W. 47
Mills, C.W. 43, 68
moderating effects 14–15, 18
Moffitt, T.E. 27, 110
moral issues
 cultural pressures in market societies 63–6
 rational choice theory 23–4
 situational-action theory 30–1
 welfare state 117–18
 see also institutions, regulation; subculture
motivations 22–3, 38, 39–40
 controls and opportunities 20–1, 23, 31–6, 102, 106–9

National Crime Victimization Survey (NCVS) 4, *5*, 12, *13*, 80
New York Times 89, 93, 94
normality of crime 56–7
'normlessness' *see* anomie
norms
 counter-norms 58
 subsystems of 56
 see also institutions, regulation
North, D.C. 55, 56

opportunities
 motivations and control 20–1, 23, 31–6, 102, 106–9
 routine activities and 37–40

organized crime 88–93
 definition 78

parental/family attachment 34, 35
parochial controls 44
Parsons, T. 55, 58, 62
performance, institutional 59–60, 62–3, 77–86, 108–9
Polanyi, K. 60, 71, 117, 118
policy change *vs* social change 99–106
population heterogeneity 40–1, 42
poverty *see* socioeconomic status
price changes 80–1
 inflation 81–3, 85–6
 'trading down' 83–4
Pridemore, W.A.
 et al. 75–6
 and Kim, S.-W. 76–7
prison system 100–6
prisoners
 drug offences 93
 ethnicity 104
 socioeconomic status 3
private controls 44
Prohibition 89
property/acquisitive crime 10–13
 burglary *5*, 16–17
 see also routine activities
 and homicides 10–12
 and inflation 81–3
 stolen goods 83–6
 theft 12–13
Protestant Ethic 65
proximate causes of crime 106–9
public controls 44

race *see* ethnicity
rational choice theory 21–4
  extensions and
    reformulations 24–31
regulation, institutional 58–9,
  63–6, 73–7, 108–9, 115–19
residential instability 42
Rosenfeld, R. 10–12, 79,
  106, 114
  Blumstein, A. and 90
  et al. 5, *6*
  and Fornango, R. 79
  and Messner, S.F. 14, 100
  Messner, S.F. and 29, 46–7,
    55, 61, 72, 101, 117
Rothstein, B. 117
routine activities 37–40
rules of the game 56, 57,
  58–60, 63–4, 76, 78
Rushe, G. and Kirchheimer, O.
  100–1
Russia, post-Soviet 73–7

Sampson, R.J.
  et al. 6–7, 37, 44–5
  and Laub, J.H. 34
  and Lauritsen, J.L. 4
Schwartz, B. 62, 96–7
self-control 25–6, 30–1, 35
sentencing policies 101–2, 103
Shaw, C. and McKay, H.D. 37,
  41–3, 44
Sherman, M. 95, 96
Simon, J. 101
situational-action theory (SAT)
  30–1, 34–5
social bond theory 29, 34, 43
social change *vs* policy change
  99–106
social control
  disorganized communities
    and 40–5

social control *cont.*
  erosion of 62–3
  theories 29, 43
  types of 44
social institutions *see*
  institutions
social learning theory 27–8, 33
  see also subculture
social psychological theories
  26, 27–31, 32–3
social systems 55–6
social welfare provisions 71–3,
  117–18
  cross-national comparison
    14–15, 72–3
  Russia 75–6
socialization 24–5, 34,
  35, 69
socioeconomic status 2–7, 33,
  34, 35, 36–7, 38–9, 47
  see also household income
Stanley, A. 74
stolen goods 83–6
street crime 79–83
  definition 78
structure, institutional 58, 60,
  61, 62, 70–3
subculture 43, 45–7, 48–9
subsystems of norms 56
suburbanization of white
  population 51
Sullivan, M.L. 91
supply and demand 111–14
Sutton's Law 1–2, 13

theft 12–13
'trading down' 83–4

unemployment 3, 39, 40,
  49–50, 83, 85–6
  homicides and welfare
    system 14–15, 72

unemployment *cont.*
  vs other economic indicators
    79–80
Uniform Crime Reports (UCR)
  80, 81
unmediated/direct effect
  7–8, *9*

victimization
  socioeconomic status 4, *5*,
    12–13, 16–17
  violent subculture 46
violence 85, 92–3, 114
  antisocial behaviour in
    juveniles 110–11, 112
  firearms 90

violence *cont.*
  and property crime 10–12
  and socioeconomic status 33
  subculture 46
  see also homicides
Void, G.B. 2

Weber, M. 65
welfare *see* social welfare
    provisions
white flight 51
white-collar crime 93–7
  definition 78
Wikström, P-O.H. 30–1, 34–5
Wilson, W.J. 48, 49–52, 101
Wrong, D.H. 24–5